GOD IN MY LIFE

Faith Stories and How and Why We Share Them

Maren C. Tirabassi & Maria I. Tirabassi

THE PILGRIM PRESS
CLEVELAND

The Pilgrim Press, 700 Prospect Avenue, Cleveland, Ohio 44115-1100
thepilgrimpress.com
© 2008 by Maren C. Tirabassi, Maria I. Tirabassi

13   12   11   10   09   08   5   4   3   2

Library of Congress Cataloging-in-Publication Data

Tirabassi, Maren C.
    God in my life : faith stories and how and why we share them / Maren C. Tirabassi & Maria I. Tirabassi.
        p. cm.
    Includes indexes.
    ISBN 978-0-8298-1779-9 (alk. paper)
    1. Christian teenagers—Religious life.   2. Young adults—Religious life.   3. Storytelling—Religious aspects—Christianity. I. Tirabassi, Maria I., 1983–   II. Title.
    BV4531.3.T57 2008
    248.8'3—dc22   2008005075

❖ CONTENTS ❖

MY SCOTTISH GRANDMOTHER, Ruth Elizabeth Rankin, shared with me a lesson from her mother, Anna McArthur. She said, "If you want to know a people, you must know the stories they tell." This has been a guiding principle in my own work, as I have explored storytelling over the years. I have always loved stories, be they folk or fairy tales, fables, animal tales, myths and legends, or, of course, personal stories in which people seek to make meaning of their own lives and experiences. In these stories, people do what has been done since the beginning of time: they try to understand who we are, whose we are, and why we are here. We discover who we are in the telling and the hearing of our stories. In this collection of stories we find contemporary Christian folk making sense of how they came to be who they are here and now.

When I first heard about *God in My Life: Faith Stories and How and Why We Share Them,* I thought, "OMG! (Oh, my God)! This is just what we need—a book that presents people's faith journeys to the world. For years, I have had an opportunity to work with people in faith settings in the United Church of Christ and beyond to help them provide a place to tell parts of their faith stories out loud. I have experienced first hand the power that comes in remembering one's story, the sense of joy, satisfaction, and connection that comes from telling that story to another and having it received. Listening is the other half of telling—just as reading is the other half of writing. Maren Tirabassi and Maria

Tirabassi have gracefully invited people to reflect on important moments in their lives, in which they experienced God, a sacred space, or a faith challenge, and to write those stories down. Those stories are in this book. What an important and timely gift. People are hungry for stories. And this book offers a feast.

You will read stories that touch your heart, cause you to catch your breath, make you think, and laugh with tears in your eyes. These tales come from young people, lay people, pastors, and conference ministers, all human beings willing to bear witness to their experiences. Be careful. You may find yourself nodding your head, thinking, "I remember when . . ." If you do, do not worry. Maren and Maria have provided clear, step-by-step tools for you to use when that desire for story sharing takes over. So often people will say, "I don't have a story to tell." Or "what happened to me wasn't important." Of course, that's not true. We sometimes just need guidance for uncovering those memories and suggestions as to how to share them in ways that honor the teller, the tale, and the listeners. This book will help you tell your own story, and help you help others tell stories, too. There are creative ideas for story prompts. For those who tremble at the idea of literally writing things down, there are wonderful alternatives to pen and paper. I can't wait to try writing on a banana peel! There are even suggestions for sharing that use storytelling, print, new lyrics to old songs, or PowerPoint.

I was born and raised in a Congregational church in New England. It was full of faithful people whose lives reflected their beliefs, and who generally didn't talk about it much. I didn't know what "testimony" was until I experienced more diverse churches. There I saw the power of the story, and the telling, on the community. I remembered my great-grandmother's words, "If you want to know a people, you must know the stories they tell." No wonder Jesus told the disciples to go out and share the good news. He knew the power of story. In this soul-thirsty world full of seekers, we need more than ever to remember that God is still speaking, every day, to and through many people, in many ways. This book is proof of that.

Valerie Tutson, storyteller, of Stories 'n Stuff

INTRODUCTION
lovetotellstories@gmail.com

AND PEOPLE DO—love to tell stories about themselves and their experience of God. In fact, they are just waiting to be asked!

That was the e-mail address for this book, *God In My Life: Faith Stories and How and Why We Share Them*—and for about six months amazing stories flowed in to that site.

We began in June 2007 with an invitation to conference ministers in the United Church of Christ and the leadership of the six historically underrepresented groups to write a two-hundred- to four-hundred-word story about a time when God was real and vital in their own teenaged years. Some of these folks delegated the writing to a colleague in ministry or a well-known pastor or lay leader. In addition, each was invited to find a young person in the conference or affinity group to respond to our invitation with a similar story. Here are some of the "writing prompts" they received:

In the midst of natural beauty, I felt God's presence . . .

On Christmas Eve or Easter dawn the Bible came alive . . .

Somebody nurtured me in faith . . .

I faced a fork in the road . . .

When a friend was engaged in risky behavior—cutting, drinking, bingeing, starving, etc.—I felt God's guidance . . .

I knew I was called to ministry when . . .

I was empowered to speak out as a prophet when . . .

On a mission experience, I knew that God was telling me . . .

When I felt alone or abandoned, I sensed something beyond myself. . . . There's a "thin place," a mysterious experience . . .

After a death, I felt vulnerable and . . .

When I was angry with God . . .

We received at least one story that reflected each one of these ideas and a wide range of wonderful unanticipated stories. A few generalizations are possible. Clearly outdoor ministries are absolutely central to the vitality of the United Church of Christ. If you want someone to grow up to become a conference minister—send him or her to camp! God is experienced through mentors, guides, "saints"—likely and unlikely ones. There are Sarges and Annies and Toms out there who are changing lives though they may never know it. Some of these stories reflect on choosing or "unchoosing" a vocation, choosing or unchoosing a personal relationship, hearing the call of conscience, recognizing injustice, or speaking out to change the world or the church. Many writers describe the fragile openness of times of loss and grief and how God's tenderness is experienced directly or through the comfort of others.

Here are a few practical points as you read this book. For convenience, we divided the book into five broad themes, but, as the reader browses, it will be obvious that many of the seventy pieces fit into two or three different chapters. There are some stories that run more than four hundred words—in all those cases the original manuscript was significantly longer.

We made the decision to identify each writer in this book by name and affiliation. We chose not to disclose which writings were by the younger participants and which were by the older ones. Content will indicate age in some cases. The younger writers ranged from fourteen to twenty years of age. In correspondence with a youth group leader from Cuba I mentioned this project, and many months later a number of "unsolicited submissions" arrived. Touched by the group's enthusiasm, we have included one in each age category and they are marked Pentecostal Church of Cuba. Thanks goes to Ellen Fries for her translation.

The book closes with a brief resource section of ways small group facilitators can invite participants of any age to write, speak, or otherwise share stories. Many youth leaders invite the sharing of faith stories as a regular and rich part of the community life. These people may not need our pragmatic suggestions. In fact, an anthology of best methods for talking about faith would be a wonderful thing! This section is offered as a resource of simple activities and a "spelling out" of things we instinctively know about safe and effective sharing.

Readers have free permission to use and adapt these resources. Please reprint the faith stories as well for congregational use! Credit each writer and the book when you do so.

We are honored to have been trusted with these stories. What a joy! Thanks to every contributor and to a number of unnamed youth ministers who helped and encouraged the participation of young people. Thanks as well to Kim Martin Sadler, our editor with The Pilgrim Press, who always inspires us in the writing of books and makes us laugh! Thanks to the National Youth Event planning committee for the invitation to put a book together for the event and for liking our idea. We appreciate once again the creative teamwork of Kristin Firth and Rick Porter in copyediting and layout. We give them a jumble and it comes back a joy. We are grateful to our amazing and supportive families and friends.

Maybe our relationship with God is like this; we are unsteady and doubtful until we alight safely on the ground. Then we look around, and see that the people around us have acted out God's divine presence in our lives. Maybe that's what grace is—the hands that hold us up when we can't support ourselves. Who are you supporting, and who is supporting you?

Lucia Hulsether of the Southeast Conference of the United Church of Christ wrote these words. We agree. That is the intention of this book—to be a celebration of grace and a source of grace, to testify to the ways in which people are supported, and even to hope the stories themselves strengthen, inspire, and support those who read them!

Maren C. Tirabassi
Maria I. Tirabassi

FAITH STORIES

1   GRACE ENCOUNTERS

I LEARNED THE TRUTH AT SEVENTEEN

That's the first line of a popular Janis Ian song from 1975, but also an accurate statement from my life. I was seventeen years old and I was on a big date with my new girlfriend. We were attending a concert with my parents (okay, so I was a nerd). In the middle of the concert, my father suffered a massive heart attack, flopped across my date's lap, and died.

That was the end of what had been a tranquil, predictable life.

The one constant throughout this experience was my girlfriend, Ann. She was at my side when I just needed a presence. She was there to hold me when I needed to cry. Ann provided a safe place for me. Five years later we were married.

"And they lived happily ever after."

Hardly. Life has not been a happily-ever-after affair. We had a stillborn child who never had the chance to breathe or know the love that had been waiting for her. We had a child diagnosed with leukemia who suffered untold agonies from cancer treatments before he was cured. And ten years ago I was the victim of a hit-and-run accident that left me in a wheelchair, paralyzed below the waist. We sometimes huddle together and wonder, "What's next?"

The truth that was revealed to me at seventeen? You might think I'd be bitter about life by now. Just look at the bad things that have happened. But the truth that I began learning in high school is just the opposite. Life is precious. The world is a grand mystery waiting to be explored. In addition to the tragedies, we have lived some remarkable adventures along the way that I wouldn't have traded for the world. There is no moment so dark that it can't be illuminated by God's grace. God doesn't keep us from harm, but God does offer grace to help us pick up the pieces and go on. Like a friend who stands by you when you're in pain, God's heart breaks when we suffer. For me, that's enough.

Robert Molsberry, Ohio Conference

A LITTLE GAME

In the summer of 2007 I had the chance to go on a mission trip to Tanzania. I went with my father and several people from my church. I thought that in Tanzania I would be sharing God's love through talking and praying or through painting buildings and generally helping out. In fact, I found that one of the ways I was able to most fully share God's love with others was through a simple game of soccer. Soccer is so amazing because all you need to play is a ball and a couple of people. Anyone can join in and play. This leads to a community where all different sorts of people who don't even speak the same language can meet each other and become friends. This game came to show me a bit of God's power and love in action.

When I got to the village of Pommern, Tanzania, I immediately went outside and pulled out a hacky-sack. The children were amazed at first to see such a thing but after a couple of minutes they moved me on to a game of soccer. Once the soccer ball came out we played nonstop; we played soccer at night and in the day. When I got up in the morning the kids would be waiting outside my door. We became great friends through the game of soccer.

Just before I left Tanzania I received a note from one of my soccer friends. He wrote in broken English, "to mi friend Alex. Thanks for teaching me to play soccer." Upon receiving this note, I nearly cried. I had sought to share God's love with them and they had so shared it with me. The amazing thing was that I did not know any of these children's names or speak their language. But the connection I made with them because of this little game was indescribable. When I left Tanzania I wanted to bring back this sense of community that I had experienced. I am still working on doing that. I think God wants all of us to be open to meeting new and different people and all the joys that come from these experiences. From my time in Tanzania I learned that God's love can be found in the most unlikely of places even in something as simple as a game of soccer.

Alex Cook, Massachusetts Conference

GOD IS ABLE TO PROVIDE YOU WITH EVERY BLESSING IN ABUNDANCE

During the civil rights movement in the 1960s, mean-spirited southern officials provided poor African American males with one-way bus tickets to northern cities, like Cleveland. They were called reverse freedom riders.

It was summertime. My birthday. My father suggested that this year's celebration be dinner at a new, special, popular restaurant. My mother and boyfriend agreed that this was the way to celebrate. This new restaurant was the talk of the town. I was so excited. I could not wait.

My father, a photojournalist, called during the day to tell me that the first reverse freedom riders were coming to Cleveland that evening. He wanted to capture the moment before we went to celebrate. I agreed.

That evening, we met three young men at the Greyhound bus station, each carrying a shoebox containing all their worldly possessions. They were polite, quiet, and not really certain why they were there. But all were convinced that the decision to come to the north was the opportunity for a better life.

We soon learned they had not eaten that day. We took them into the bus station restaurant and told them to order whatever they wanted to eat. As they ate, we sat and talked and learned a little about them and their dreams and aspirations.

After several hours, we prepared to leave. Shelter had been arranged for them by a local social service agency. We prayed with them and went on our way.

As we began to drive to the restaurant for what would now be a late dinner, I said I no longer wanted to go. In my mind, the money my father spent for the reverse freedom riders dinner was his gift to me to use for "the least of these." I felt so good that my parents had always taught me to share. I felt so good that God has always provided everything and more in my life. There was nothing else I wanted.

Yes. I was my brother's keeper. Yes. I knew how to do unto others.

That day I celebrated my birthday in a different way. No gifts to me. No gifts for me.

Gifts for "the least of these."

In the midst of celebration, God reaffirmed God's goodness. In the midst of celebration, I was a witness.

You can't beat God's giving,
no matter how you try . . . .
The more you give,
the more He give to you,
but keep on giving

because it's really true
that you can't beat God's giving,
no matter how you try. (by Doris Akers, 1957, Manna Music)

Carol A. Brown, United Black Christians

FINDING FAITH . . .

My fifth-grade year was off to a good start, except I was lacking one thing—friends. As the seating chart would have it, I was sitting next to the other person in the class who also didn't have friends at school. She was new to public school as she had been home-schooled to that point. Right off, we became good friends. As the year passed we realized our similarities, and our friendship grew deeper. She once mentioned that she was going to youth group at her church. She told me how much fun she had and about all the great people that she knew through her church. I was curious; I had been to church on the holidays and occasionally to Sunday school, but youth group? What was that?

As time went on, she influenced me greatly. Soon enough, she had me listening to the Christian rock station that she listened to. She often taught me about the message in the lyrics and what it meant to her. One day in our conversation, I asked a question, and she referred to the Bible for the answer.

I wasn't quite sure what to think. I had never read the Bible before and certainly didn't understand the words that she read to me. Her solution to this was to bring me to her youth group, which I later realized was a Bible study. During the lesson I was taught of steps that I could take to clean my soul.

This was one of many lessons that were emphatically preached to me; however, it wasn't the individual lessons that impacted me most. It was the community and the sense of love among the people that intrigued me. As time wore on I began to attend my own church more frequently and I became more involved. I soon discovered that the church that my friend attended had very different theological perspectives than the church that my family attended; nevertheless, the community and sense of love were the same.

In retrospect, what my friend had given me was more than her friendship. What the lessons had taught me was more than scripture alone could speak. What I had found was my faith.

Chelsea E. Bicknell, Maine Conference

A NEW GIFT

Since the day I was born, God has been an important character to (literally) look up to. Growing up as a minister's daughter in the church it seems as if God has always been present in my life, in some way or another; but more specifically, there are always the moments that I'm lost and confused, with no place to turn, and there, I know God is present. I moved to Los Angeles, California, two weeks after I graduated from high school. I went from homemade dinners and free clothes to electric bills and insane traffic. After my mother and father waved me off to be on my own, I felt lost. My overall goal, and the reason for moving, was to further my career in the professional world of acting in film and television, but where was I supposed to start, and how was I supposed to survive before my dream became a reality?

Sitting alone in my new apartment, smelling fresh paint and seeing boxes galore, it occurred to me that I wasn't really lost. No matter what, I wasn't completely alone. What I had learned and studied in church slowly came back into my mind:

"Even though I walk through the darkest valley, I fear no evil; for you are with me; your rod and your staff—they comfort me" (Ps. 23).

The Divine Shepherd God was always going to be on my side, through thick and thin. Two days later, I was working as a background actor for the very first time. I was nervous, scared, and anxious to be on an actual television set. Then out of nowhere an old friend whom I'd met in California one year before at a workshop walked through the door. Since then, we haven't left each other's side. I thank God for everything that I get put through because I know that it makes me a stronger person in the end. Without God's presence, it gets hard to let the light in on a rainy day, but with God's presence, I shine.

Martha Brigham, California, Nevada Southern Conference

OPEN DOOR . . . TO ME

The San Francisco Bay area is notorious for its unpredictable weather. Summers, especially in San Francisco, are short, and autumn, winter, and spring may as well be one separate season of varying wind and rain.

It was during one of those autumn/winters that our youth group volunteered their Saturday to work the soup kitchen for a church in San Francisco. If I remember correctly, this was between Thanksgiving and Christmas, when the season became busy with Christmas shopping, parties, and hinting wish lists to our parents. Needless to say, some of us had our mind on other things.

But being that this was the holiday season, I expected to come away with a good feeling for doing my part to help the community. That was all I expected.

We arrived that morning to a bustle of activity. The regular volunteer staff were already scrambling around the kitchen prepping and cooking food. We would be prepping plates and serving the line.

We were a somber group as we entered, feeling slightly guilty for having food in our stomachs and nice, clean clothes to wear, and anticipating a quiet, sullen crowd. So what a surprise to be greeted with beaming faces, to see people in line for food with more morning energy than many of us could possibly muster on a midweek school morning. I couldn't help but smile and hold back my own emotions, instead choosing to feed off the positive energy from many in the room. Things I stressed about earlier in my week seemed so trivial as I saw people gathered by a piano, belting out songs as the guy at the seat banged out tune after tune. The message of faith was apparent on many of their faces, despite the knowledge that soon they would again be braving the elements and a not always kind community. But here in the shelter they and I found a peace so easy to forget, and a time to thank God and our brothers and sisters for showing each other that we are not alone and God will always send us small miracles to take care of us.

Sharon Encabo Seegmiller, Pacific Islanders and Asian American Ministries

ABSALOM

As a junior in high school, I began to attend church at the invitation of a friend. Early on, I found in the minister a model of everything I hoped I could be in my life. Life and the education for ministry have meant revisiting this sense of vocation many times from many angles. I certainly know that the experience was far more complex than it seemed in the imagination of the boy I was then.

One Sunday morning, my pastor was preaching on the death of Absalom. As he reenacted David's tears and transformed them into God's tears at the loss of all who go astray, I felt God near. No matter what I had heard about God, I couldn't imagine that kind of grief or affection from a father. Time has taught me that affection is often there in ways that aren't apparent at the time. But the image of David crying for Absalom and God weeping for all the lost children of the world brought God into my heart in a powerful way. My whole life and belief found its footing that day.

Roddy Dunkerson, Nebraska Conference

A FRESH START

I know God is real. I don't know what you believe. Maybe what I say will help you see some small touches in this world that are guided by God.

My sophomore year in high school, I was the stereotypical bookworm who turned in all assignments on time and answered all the questions right. I had long, gorgeous blonde hair and a small frame, and I met a guy. We were in band together and he was eight months younger than me. I fell for him hard. I liked him and he liked me, for a little while at least. He dumped me a month later for no reason, straight out of the blue. I was heartbroken. Things started looking up, though, when he asked me back out just three weeks later. He broke up with me again, this time for one of my friends, who shot him down.

I looked at myself and I wondered: Who am I? Why? I was quiet because I was scared; I read because I had no friends; I wanted a guy because I had no confidence or self-love.

Then, I found love. Not from a guy, but from God. I really found meaning in the passage "I can do all things through Christ who strengthens me." I came to believe in it strongly. I left my shell. I started hanging out and making friends with people from all walks of life. I stepped outside of my "box" and listened to new music, read new books, tried new looks. I cut thirteen inches off my hair and donated it to Locks of Love. I was a new person. I knew that no matter what anyone thought, God would still love and comfort me. God gave me the reasons to be myself.

Courtney Monzyck, Missouri Mid-South Conference

A FAITH JOURNEY BEGINS

I suppose it was one of the least likely places to get redirected and inspired, but my first exposure into the academic study of the New Testament during my sophomore year in college proved to be just that for me. The setting was not necessarily conducive to faith development. The approach to the subject matter was analytical and historical. The expectation was that we students would learn about the New Testament from the standpoint of critical scholarship. Yet, for me, the gospel message came alive and grabbed my attention like it never had in my years growing up in church or around Christian people.

Mind you, this was the mid-1960s and my college, Lincoln University in Pennsylvania, was populated for the most part by African American males. The school had only enrolled its first cadre of resident female students in my freshman class. The social environment was rude and crude, as we often liked to characterize it. So, you can imagine just how unlikely it would be that anyone would openly espouse religious belief or spiritual aspiration or openly display any sense of piety. Of course, there were a few such brave souls, but they were usually held up for playful ridicule or simply regarded with a benign incredulity.

There was a standing joke at Lincoln about our New Testament Professor, Dr. Davies. People said that if you went to one of his lectures, you got the sense that he was standing right there with Jesus when Jesus gave the Sermon on the Mount. I guess my story is wrapped up in the joke. You see, Dr. Davies, while walking us through the ins and outs of critical analysis and historical contexts, was aglow with the Spirit, God's Holy Spirit. He simply loved to tell the story and without his uttering a word of belief or invitation, the joy and authenticity of his faith was compelling. Without ever knowing it, Dr. Davies had opened my heart and mind to the gospel. The experience was transformative, but, remember, I was at Lincoln University in 1967. So quietly, very quietly, I began to take the journey of faith, and I am still on that journey today.

Geoffrey A. Black, New York Conference

RACHEL'S TEARS

Looking back at a time when I needed spiritual awakening, I realize that I got it from a person that I never met. A few days post–September 11, 2001, an adult in my church, Raul, handed me a booklet of people expressing their grief at the tragic events concerning that day through their stories and poems. I came across a poem by Darrell Scott and he mentioned losing his daughter, Rachel Scott, due to something out of his control. Rachel was killed during the Columbine High School shootings. Since I was unfamiliar about this event, I did some research online and found a book by Darrell called *Rachel's Tears*. I bought the book and I came to find that Rachel was an ordinary teenager who did extraordinary things because she had a very close relationship with God and took her faith seriously.

Rachel Scott inspired me. Because of her, sometimes when I feel down, I write journal entries to God. I have become unashamed of expressing my belief in God to others. Rachel used to love theater and she was the person who got me interested in that form of art. Ever since eighth grade, I have found that I've had a passion for it and it has become a way for me to get out of my comfort zone and express myself. I find it amazing how much of a difference one person can make in your life. Rachel once wrote in an essay, "I have a theory that if one person can go out of their way to show compassion, then it will start a chain reaction of the same." She restored my faith and she reminded me to live life fully or optimistically towards others and myself, because life can be taken away at anytime. It's a unique blessing to realize how much you can be spiritually attuned to others.

Michelle Santiago, Pacific Islanders and Asian American Ministries,
California, Nevada Northern Conference

STRIDER

A little over two years ago, I found a strange bump on the side of my horse's mouth. The results of a biopsy came back saying it was a sarcoid tumor, something very common and harmless in horses. I kept watching the bump, and in the course of a week it had doubled in size and had become hard. We trailered him up to NC State's Veterinary Hospital, where they did a second biopsy. That is when my world came crashing down.

That little bump wasn't a harmless sarcoid tumor, but a coetaneous fibroid sarcoma. Cancer in horses is rare, and this is the rarest form. I was strong in the barn in front of my mom. I lost it when I went outside.

The first thought that crossed my mind was "Why is God doing this to me?" Suddenly I felt a nudge on my shoulder. Strider had followed me. I wrapped my arms around his neck, praying it wouldn't be the last time I did so. Frowning into his thick winter fur I turned my head to the side. Looking up at the sky and the setting sun, I prayed. Prayed for Strider, prayed for me to be strong, prayed for the vets who would be taking care of him.

A few weeks later Strider started chemotherapy. About three months after that we took him up to NC State again to have the tumor removed. It had grown in size again because it had started feeding off of the chemo. The entire time that he was sick, I felt as if I had a friend by my side, pulling me along. Someone was helping me to stay strong as I made my way through this maze. God was right there beside me and Strider. Today Strider is cancer free and back to the horse he was before all of this. This is just one time when I felt God's presence, and I will never forget it.

Brittany H. Rogers, Southern Conference

PLEASE, I NEED TO KNOW

Last year a boy transferred into my high school. The student head of the theatre tech crew introduced him to me as a great guy. He was well known for his lighting design back home. I was psyched for someone with some decent experience to join us.

Once he joined the school, people started to think that we were dating because we spent a lot of time together. Whether we were a couple or not, I cared about him. Unfortunately, shortly after he started school, rumors about him started. My friends were telling me that he was trouble and that I should stop seeing him, and one of them was the same boy who had introduced him to me. I was confused and had no idea who to believe. The people telling me this had been my friends for years and I felt bad for not trusting them, but I had gotten to know him and I couldn't believe what they said. As a last resort I prayed. I asked God to please, please, tell me what I should do. The next day the boy found me and explained everything to me.

I thought that it would blow over, but the tech head still hated the new guy for what he supposedly had done. I tried to convince him and a few others that this guy was perfectly nice, and that he deserved a second chance, even if he had made a mistake. The tech head and I ended up not talking for a long time after he told someone how it was obvious that "that bastard" and I were dating even if we did deny it, and that I was so stupid to hang out with him. I prayed again because both boys were good friends. In prayer, I realized that I was being a hypocrite. I had told the tech head to forgive the boy that he wouldn't talk to, but afterwards, I had stopped talking to him for something I wouldn't forgive him for.

Before that, I had never prayed for something that I really needed to know, and I was shocked at how fast the turnaround was. In each case, I had a moment of "Eureka!" the next day when each of them found me and helped me see what I had to do. The new boy showed me how he was still a good kid, no matter what people were saying, and the tech head found me and tried to apologize, while showing me that I needed to apologize too. I pray for guidance more often now that I know that it helps me to see what I need to do.

Rachel B. Axtell, Vermont Conference

ONE GOD FITS ALL

God works in mysterious ways and it is indeed by no mistake that I'm writing this. While I rarely know what to write or the words to use, I feel God definitely guides me to a message that could never possibly come from me alone. It is not only this, but all things in my life that God guides me through. Each and every day I am amazed at the wonders provided for us, God's beloved children. Many things that people take for granted are God's gifts to this world. I experience God every time I see the sun rise, hear a newborn baby crying, or feel God's embracing touch as the wind swirls around me. Not a thing in the world is without God.

As God constantly displays these signs of love, I also experience this on a much more personal level. I always turn to God for the strength and courage I need to continue through the day. When I am fearful, sad, or even angry, I lift my troubles to God in prayer and feel comforted. Even in times of abandonment, God is by my side. When life is overwhelming, and I can't seem to find the path I need to follow, God provides me with signs necessary to put me back on track.

It goes without mentioning that at times I have followed the wrong path and sinned. However, God generously forgives any sins committed by those who seek forgiveness. While I feel unworthy of God's everlasting mercy, it is God's unyielding love for me and for all humanity that saves me from my own shortcomings.

Tesa Miles, Nebraska Conference

A KNOCK AT THE DOOR

When I was a high school youth I was very sure of where I was headed in life. I was a college student majoring in Business Administration and sure that I would be successful in whatever business I would enter following graduation. At that time I was minimally involved in church, but a chance encounter changed my life and how I would live my life. A friend of our family was a member of a nearby UCC church. I had driven by the church often but never paid it much attention. One day the pastor of the church called my friend and wanted to visit another friend of my friend whose last name was Anderson. But my friend misunderstood and thought the pastor wanted to call on me. So they showed up at my door and invited me to their church and left. After they left, I didn't give it much thought, but a few months later, I did attend the church.

I discovered a community of believers who taught me much about church life and the love of Christ. I slowly became involved in that congregation and as a young person did just about everything—cut the church grass, helped count the offering, usher, helped with the children's Sunday school, and served on Church Council. Slowly, my certainty as what I wanted to do with my life seemed less certain. I did graduate from college and worked as an accountant for one year, but I finally decided during that year of working that God was calling me to serve in ministry. And the next year, I entered seminary.

I often think of what would have happened that day if my friend and his pastor would have called on the right person (the other friend named Anderson). Perhaps, the invitation to "come and see" what their church was all about would have never happened and I would have never had that opportunity in a small church to know that God was calling me into the ministry. The experience is a reminder to never be so certain of where I am headed and more open to where God may want me to be headed. The experience is a reminder of how God works even in those chance encounters to touch a life, change a life, direct a life. If you're certain where you're headed in life, maybe this is just a small reminder that God can work in mysterious ways to let you know where God wants you to be.

God can work in those chance encounters to let you know where you need to be.

Douglas Anders, South Central Conference

"HE LEADETH ME . . ."

"He leadeth me, O blessed thought!
O words with heavenly comfort fraught!
Whate'er I do, where'er I be,
still 'tis God's hand that leadeth me." (Joseph Gilmore, 1862)

Though they may not be as inclusive as I prefer, these words certainly ring true to my life.

I was always taught to follow my dreams and that the best way to achieve them was to have a list of steps to get there— not that I knew what those should be. A math or English assignment usually isn't too difficult, but for life decisions it becomes a bit more complicated. During high school I experienced a huge transition: instead of working towards the career I was planning on pursuing since I was five, I became more proactive in the UCC and more advanced in music—my two big passions. In pursuing these, though, I had to give up a lot of time with friends, family, and just relaxing to enjoy life. Yet something told me I was making the right decisions—I kept holding in my head the vision of what I wanted, and opportunities would appear to advance me towards that. These coincidences didn't just happen without a reason—somebody "upstairs" had to be watching out for me and helping me along my way. Jesus even said: "Oh ye of little faith—why did you not believe?" Trust in God, let God lead you, and you, too, in the words of Norman Vincent Peale, can "enjoy the blessings of a deeper faith and face the difficulties of life with courage and confidence."

"He leadeth me, he leadeth me,
by his own hand he leadeth me;
his faithful follower I would be,
for by his hand he leadeth me."

Kevin Peterson, Pacific Northwest Conference

REMEMBERING THE HILLTOP . . .

It was in the early spring of 1975 that Jesus Christ came to me in a way I had not experienced him before. I was a college freshman who had sensed a call to pastoral ministry while still in high school. Yet, that call felt shallow, sometimes even contrived, in the depths of my own soul. Was this really what God wanted me to be and do with my life? The more I sought a sign of confirmation, the more it eluded me. My intellect and reason would not relieve my distress. Always I came up short of the assurance I sought. Yes, I loved the church. Yes, I loved people. Yes, I knew God loved me. But was I really called to be a minister?

I think it was in March of 1975 when I went with others to a weekend at a retreat center called "Hilltop" overlooking the Lake of the Ozarks to explore living in community with others in Christian service for the summer. On Saturday night, when the weekend was nearly ending, we sat on the carpet in the common area. Candles burned. A United Methodist pastor named Lee Whiteside offered a simple homily about our hands and the hands of Christ. He had us study our own hands, calluses, scars, and all. He encouraged us to fold our hands in prayer, to open our hands to receive God's good gifts, and use our hands to serve Christ wherever he appeared to us. Then, in the dimness, he took the bread in his hands and broke it, sharing it with the ancient words, "This is the body of Christ, broken for you. Do this in remembrance of him." Afterward, the preacher took the cup in his hands and shared it with us all. We sang a hymn. In the dimness and darkness, I cried, for in that circle of strangers and friends I had seen Jesus Christ. There I discovered the church—the same church that was present in the little village of my youth—yet a different church. I caught but a glimpse of the body of Christ in a deep, mystical reality. I rose from the table, knowing that I was indeed loved and called to be Christ's servant in ministry—to give my life, to open my heart and my hands, to live and to die for the glory of God.

I did not return to Hilltop for the summer of 1975. My journey took me elsewhere, and that is another story for another time. Twenty years later, when I was called to be a pastor in church near the Lake, I sometimes returned to Hilltop. The building was gone. A little park stood in its place. The summer community had long since disbanded. But I stood on holy ground in that thin place. On my desk to this day is stone from the hilltop, a reminder of the confirmation of my call to be Christ's disciple. And, sometimes, in the midst of the most unexpected place, Christ still appears to me, offering communion and confirmation of this call, blessing me with love and hope and peace.

Gary M. Schulte, New Hampshire Conference

SAVED BY GRACE

In my faith journey, the presence of the divine has ranged from immediate to distant, from transcendent to immanent, and from helpful to antagonistic. I have been reduced to nothing and then reformed and rebuilt as a new creation, with a new heart and new eyes. But if you asked me to relate one particular "experience" of God's presence, I would not know how to answer.

I guess I could talk about climbing a mountain and absorbing God's creation, or sharing communion at a homeless shelter, or responding to racism in my community, but I feel that God's presence in my life reaches beyond the specific and into the unknowable. And, to be perfectly honest, there are many times when I do not feel God's presence at all. And, still more honestly, right now is one of those times.

So what do we do when God is silent? How do we respond when the church is inept about the needs of youth and prayers feel like conversations with the wall? I wonder if this stillness is itself a communication. I wonder if looking back upon the "stuck times" and hard experiences of our lives, we will use hindsight and recognize God's presence in places that seemed empty before.

During a difficult period of my life, a dear friend and mentor asked me if I had ever been crowd surfing. Although my literal answer was "no," I realize that in some ways I have had this experience. My support system in times of trial has been the people around me holding me up—whether that means a stranger cheering for me at a cross-country meet or a mentor counseling me late at night. Like a crowd surfer, I do not always know whose hand is on my back, ready to catch me. My time "in the air" may not be pleasant: I may feel out of control, unsafe, or detached from the people below me. Maybe our relationship with God is like this; we are unsteady and doubtful until we alight safely on the ground. Then we look around, and see that the people around us have acted out God's divine presence in our lives. Maybe that's what grace is—the hands that hold us up when we can't support ourselves. Whom are you supporting, and who is supporting you?

Lucia L. Hulsether, Southeast Conference

2   INTO THE WILDERNESS

CLOSER TO GOD

I have been blessed with the opportunity to go on various mission trips across the state and the country. All of these experiences have impacted me in often perplexing and intriguing ways. The summer before my freshman year in high school I was able to go to the Navajo reservation up in the northeast corner of Arizona with the Shadow Rock Congregational United Church of Christ Youth Group.

This was the second time I had traveled to the Tselani Cottonwood Chapter House outside of Chinle, Arizona, and oddly enough things seemed to come together for me. It was a change in culture, and God clearly spoke to me through the feeling of community in an area where there was not much vegetation and practically barren desert. It was as if time had stopped and I was able to appreciate nature for what it truly was: a work of peaceful, serene beauty when left to thrive on its own without human interference. I also witnessed the Dine people celebrating their heritage through the art of tribal dancing, and observantly I sat in awe watching.

It seemed to me at the time that God was telling me to appreciate the simple things in my life and those closest to me to create not only an outside community but a sanctuary within myself. I realized one evening by the end of our stay on the reservation that a peaceful person is one who sees glowing beauty inside and out, and I have the vibrant sunset over the plains to thank for such an understanding.

Brittany N. Wideman, Southwest Conference

BREAKING THE RULES

I was about fourteen years old and attending a summer youth conference at Silver Lake Conference Center here in Connecticut. As usual I was having a great time with friends I'd made from earlier years and new friends that week.

We played a simulation game for an entire day that week. Those of us with blue eyes had all kinds of privileges and power. People with brown and green eyes were to be shunned and kept in their place. I played along with everyone else, but after lunch I went for a walk by myself and kept arguing with myself and with God about what we were doing by cooperating. I wanted to play differently but I didn't know whether the rules would let me. On my walk back from my special place where I always went for morning watch or other meditation times, I decided to start breaking what I thought were the rules of the game.

I don't remember all of what I did, except that I began to act differently toward the green- and brown-eyed players. I talked to them and shared my afternoon snack. The other blue-eyed people got really mad at me, but I kept on because it felt right after my quiet walk and talk with God. I look back and remember being afraid that I would lose a lot of friends and that the counselors would be angry because I was breaking the rules.

Late afternoon they brought us all together and we started to debrief the experience. "Here it comes!" I thought. At that age, I didn't like to stand out; I much preferred to be like everyone else. I didn't have much self-confidence and a lot of the time I didn't feel very good about myself. But God had put some starch in my spine that afternoon; it felt better than the morning had. My blue-eyed friends began to rant about my breaking the rules, and the others told them what it felt like to have someone with privileges take them seriously and care about what was happening to them. I blushed and ducked my head and wanted to disappear.

The year was 1958; the civil rights movement was heating up. At Silver Lake we were challenged to experience discrimination just for a day and then to think together about what it must be like to live under oppression every day of your life. When I look back over my experiences with God, this one stands out among so many others because the injection of divine starch in my spine that day gave me strength in later years when I needed to stand alone for whatever reason. I've also known God in the intimacy of worship, in quiet meditation, in the calling of the earth for its care. But the times God has been closest for me have been when I've needed strength and determination, and God has always come through!

Davida Foy Crabtree, Connecticut Conference

BREAKING NEW GROUND

Last summer when I was at church camp there was a kid in my group who was really depressed. He wasn't doing well in school, and he didn't feel like his friends had any confidence in him. His parents weren't supportive and they argued a lot. Every now and then, he had been mean to people because of things going on at home, and he felt guilty about that. He had dietary problems too. He didn't have anything or anyone he could depend on.

At first I was half in shock. You hear these stories about people whose lives are messed up, but they aren't willing to admit it. Yet here he was, saying "I have all these problems and these two people I've just met are my only two friends." I wanted to help him, but since he didn't believe in God, that took away 75 percent of my arguments that I could have used to comfort him. Luckily, my friend from church was there too. We worked together to try to help this boy.

I can't remember many of the details, since most of the conversation took place past midnight. We talked until about 2:00 in the morning. I wasn't very eloquent because it was so late, but I don't think he noticed, because he was tired too. I felt like it was really important. I remember thinking, "Wow, maybe God led me to this person, so I have to at least try to make him feel better."

Later that summer, another friend and I watched the new Noah's Ark video and had a theological discussion afterwards. He thinks everyone has at least one chance to be the best they can be. It made me think about my conversation with the kid at camp. Maybe that was my chance to guide someone. I think I did about the best that I could. Still, I worry about him sometimes. I won't see him next summer, because I'll be in the high school group. I hope he comes to camp the year after that so I can see him again.

I feel like I personally have gained a measure of confidence in my relationship with God, because here was this atheistic kid and I was able to help him a little bit. That's made me feel like God really is able to affect some things.

Henry Stone, New York Conference

THE HEAVENS ARE TELLING

It was the last night of a weeklong youth canoe trip in the remote lake country of northern Minnesota, and it was getting dark. Our group was about to participate in one of our closing rituals, the silent canoe float. This night was perfect: calm, clear, and no moon, so the stars were brilliant against the absolute darkness of the sky.

Often we had difficulty getting a group of teens, already anxious about floating in absolute dark, to abide by the rule of total quiet, but this time they got it, and the ten canoes floated silently on the glassy surface. With no wind, the stars were glittery reflections in the water.

Suddenly, beginning in the north, but quickly spreading over most of the sky, the northern lights lit up the heavens. Greens, blues, whites, pinks, all moving and pulsing across the sky, this mysterious aurora borealis visited and awed us. For nearly a full hour we floated there, alone on a boreal lake but not feeling at all alone in the world.

When nature's sky show ended, we floated back to our campsite and sat around the fire. For a long time no one needed to speak, but then one boy put into words what I imagine most of us were thinking when he said, "It was like God was speaking to us." Indeed it was. It was a transcendent moment. Nearly thirty years later I ran into a woman, now in her mid-forties, who had been one of the youth on that trip. I hadn't seen her in the intervening years, but she eagerly introduced me to her own children, saying, "This was the minister who took us on the canoe trip I talk about."

Around the campfire, we recalled the words of Psalm 19: "The heavens are telling the glory of God; and the firmament proclaims God's handiwork. Day to day pours forth speech, and night to night declares knowledge. There is no speech, nor are there words; their voice is not heard; yet their voice goes out through all the earth, and their words to the end of the world."

Sometimes in our modern world, religion and science seem to be in conflict, but there is a beautiful mystery behind both the "how" of science and the "why" of faith. The creator wants to reveal, through both mind and spirit, through all possible pathways, the saving truth of creation. God was speaking that night on a north woods lake, and for those moments we were listening, and we were changed.

David S. Moyer, Wisconsin Conference

THE "GREAT" OUTDOORS

As a member of the youth group at my church, I am given many opportunities to go out in my own community and state, and even around the country, for mission trips. This past summer I traveled with my youth group to Neon, Kentucky, a small town in eastern Kentucky in the midst of overwhelming poverty. We were working with an organization, H.O.M.E.S. (Housing Oriented Ministries Established for Service), which builds housing for low-income families and works to better the community around them.

On our day off, we drove to Breaks Interstate Park, in between Kentucky and Virginia, where we really saw the beauty of Appalachia. We took a walk to an overlook, called the Towers, and were absolutely blown away by the dense forest, the sparkling river, and the dark mountains. Our entire group stood there in awe of the beauty around us and took a moment of silence to reflect on everything we had learned so far on our mission trip. As we sat there taking in the gorgeous surroundings and natural beauty, a hawk began to circle directly overhead. As we were praying and giving thanks for such an amazing experience, the hawk continued to fly over us, and I could not help but feel the presence of God being there with us. It was an incredible feeling, almost impossible to describe, and my eyes were opened wide and my heart started to pound.

Knowing God was there with us really inspired me to truly appreciate everything that God has provided to me, from the amazing park I was at, to my opportunity to go to Kentucky and help other people. Seeing the hawk flying overhead is an experience that I remember often, especially during times when I am stressed out or concerned, and I remember that God is always watching over and always with me.

Erin Corcoran, Connecticut Conference

CALIFORNIA DREAMING

We left Santa Barbara early in the morning for what seemed like a day-long journey into very strange country to the south. Since moving to California from New Jersey I had not traveled far from my adopted hometown. I was fourteen or fifteen when a church friend and I arrived in the parking lot of a Southern California UCC church to climb aboard the ramshackle bus that would groan, rumble, and eventually die on its way up mountain roads to Pilgrim Pines. In the end we off-loaded and helped push the bus up the hill into the camp.

There, teenagers from a wide variety of backgrounds joined together for a week together with crafts, Bible study, volleyball, more volleyball, skits, and swimming. We hiked up the mountain and closed out our days at Vesper Point singing as we watched the bright orange sun set through the haze of southern California's smog. It was there for the first time that I met kids from Watts and heard the words "civil rights." It was 1960.

At the end of the week I was invited back later that summer for UCC Youth Fellowship leadership camp. Through leadership camp and other similar experiences my faith and self-confidence grew. Without really knowing what I was getting into, I joined the conference's youth cabinet, which met throughout the year in Pasadena.

Looking back from today's perspective I am very grateful that my parents and various youth group advisors saw something in me that showed potential. I hope that today as a conference minister in the Central Atlantic Conference for the past fifteen years I have lived up to their expectations. They gave me a marvelous gift.

John Deckenback, Central Atlantic Conference

FROM HAPPINESS TO DESPAIR TO REAL JOY

I had an insanely happy childhood. I grew up in a small town with lots of friends and lots of things to do. I had great parents and school was fun. As a matter of fact, we were so happy that my brother and I never realized that we were poor until years later.

However, in June 1971 all of the happiness ended in an instant. It was Saturday morning, my father and I were mowing the lawn, and my dad dropped over and died in my arms of a heart attack. Dad was forty-five years old and I was nineteen years old. We were loyal church-goers so I thought God would help us somehow get through the pain. But my mother was so distraught that she attempted to take her life on three different occasions.

Somehow I managed to finish college and get a job. After my first week of work as an engineer for U.S. Steel Corporation, I realized I hated the corporate world. There were so many company games to play and so much back-stabbing as people stepped on each other in an attempt to climb the ladder.

I was by then twenty-three years old, and life just felt dark: Dad had died, my mother was emotionally ill, and I had spent four years of college preparing for a career I hated.

About six months after graduation, my wife and I started going to church again— not out of faith but more out of a sense of childhood habit. The pastor at the church asked us to help with the senior-high youth group. Sunday nights became our favorite night of the week. We were supposed to be the advisors, but we were getting more out of the youth group than we felt we were giving.

In February 1975, the pastor asked us to help chaperone the annual senior-high youth retreat. I had never been on a retreat; I didn't know what to expect. The pastor spent the weekend trying to help us experience "koinonia," the fellowship enjoyed by those drawn into community by Christ. We played silly games, we shared during relational Bible studies, we had a bizarre talent show, we laughed, we ate, and we sang. On the closing night the pastor had us sit in a circle. He then invited anyone who wanted to share a word with the group. Some shared words of "thanks" for a great weekend. Others shared stories of things they had to face back home and asked the group to pray for them. After each person shared their words, they were invited to sit in the middle of the circle while we laid hands on them and prayed for them. Suddenly I began to speak, although it was hard to talk through my sobs. I told of my father's death, my mother's illness, and my disillusionment with my career. When it was over no one said anything, for there was nothing to say. But everyone stayed with me and did not leave me alone with my pain.

The next morning when I woke up, I felt like my soul had just had a bath. I remember thinking: "I wonder if life as I had been experiencing it was the result of the way we humans had messed up God's creative desire for us; and I wonder if what I had experienced in that circle last night was the way that God had created us to live and to love one another." For the first time in my life I had found meaning and purpose—I had found God.

Alan C. Miller, Pennsylvania Northeast Conference

A LARGER AUDIENCE

Music has always been a defining factor in my life. I have innumerable early memories of riding in the car and my family bursting out into raucous song. Singing seemed a convenient way to pass the time. It wasn't until I was older that I realized not all families spontaneously sang in the car. But I couldn't imagine it any other way.

This love of music carried over into my church life. I anticipated every hymn and chorus. Even if I couldn't read all the words, the tunes were familiar. The music I heard gave me an instinctive sense of solace. And gradually I began to appreciate the meaning behind the lyrics.

With my understanding of church music, my own musical abilities began to flourish. When I started to play the piano, one of my first lesson books was one of common Christian melodies. Excitedly I learned that I could play for myself some of the songs I had heard in church that Sunday. My parents encouraged my musical tendencies and one summer sent me off to a music-themed church camp. Once I arrived, I loved camp. Everyone sang in the choir, some kids played instruments in the band, but most of all we shared a love for music.

A concert would be performed at the end of the week when the parents came to retrieve their children. It seemed the perfect way for all of us to show our moms and dads what we had done that week. I was then given a reminder that I'll never forget. "We perform for an audience of one," I was told. "It's a small way to give thanks to our God." I kept that in mind that night when I sang, and rather than trying to impress my parents, my song was a prayer I could relate to.

I'm a little older today. My family that used to sing in the car now sings for church audiences. The hymns I played out of that beginner's book ended up being a useful part of my repertoire—I frequently play during my church service. And each year I've gone back to camp, I still sing. All of this music serves one purpose, to glorify God. Because as much as I love music, I know God loves it even more when I return the credit back to where it belongs.

Rachel McDonald, Pennsylvania West Conference

WE WERE ALL WET!

The rain was slamming down in buckets. We were twenty-three young adults. We were four days into an eight-day hike through the Pecos Wilderness in New Mexico. As we were about to navigate a narrow mountain pass, a cowboy came by to warn us: rain was coming. The sun shone bright: we almost ignored him. Wisely, we chose to listen.

Hours of torrential rain followed. By the end of the afternoon sleeping bags were soaked; tents filled with inches of rain; jackets proved fruitless.

In the hours that followed, I witnessed something I shall never forget.

Instead of whining, complaining, and bemoaning our circumstances—we rallied. The sun returned in the late afternoon sky, and rainbows covered the range. Firewood was found; dinner cooked. Sleeping bags wrung out gallons of water and were hung over the fire as the sun set, the cool night air enveloped us, the stars emerged.

Before we all fell into the blissful slumber that came gratefully to us at the end of each long day, we sat around the fire sharing our thoughts, sharing our prayers, singing with renewed vigor.

Tomorrow would bring a whole new set of challenges; but knowing we had met this one changed us. And as the stars grew closer in the night air we each reflected on the pride that came to us, the self-confidence that was now ours to own and claim for having learned just how resilient we could be, for coming to know the value of building community in adversity, and for finding a new and better place in which the voice of God could be heard.

John C. Dorhauer, Missouri Mid-South Conference

THE BEST AND HARDEST PART

Love. It's such a simple word and such a complicated thing. The time I fell in love might have been the only time I thought I had things figured out. Here begins a traditional summer romance . . .

We met counseling at church camp. Our friendship developed and we found ourselves suddenly in love. Inseparable as we were the rest of the summer, it seemed that nothing could go wrong. I was reluctant, having been hurt before, but I couldn't deny him; it was the type of love that would carry you to the ends of time if you gave it half a chance.

College came. The summer "honeymoon" was over, and it was back to reality. Because we were attending different schools, a thousand miles separated us like a vast ocean. At first we scoffed at this arbitrary obstacle that dared threaten our bond.

Though apart, we dreamt together what the future could hold. The prospect of spending the rest of our lives together was consuming. It didn't even seem illogical to be thinking these things . . . the future is all you have when you're in a long-distance relationship.

The months passed. Frustration set in as we were unable to share our day-to-day lives. We began to lose sight of each other, how we felt, even why we were in the relationship to begin with.

The plot couldn't have been more predictable. He became depressed, unable to cope with the distance. I felt betrayed, having been hurt again by this thing called "love." It became nothing more than a ruse to me, a tool used to hurt. I had finally let my guard down only to be cut even deeper. *I should have seen it coming*, I thought.

We broke up before I went abroad for three months. The change of location helped distract me, but I clung to bitter memories. This resentment truly amounted to my lingering love, but it was easier to lay blame than to own up to what I really felt. After all, if *he* didn't still feel love, then *I* didn't want to either.

By the time I got home it had been months since we'd talked and I thought I had finally come to terms with the situation.

Summer returned, and with it came camp. I was hopeful that would be a healing time for me. What I didn't count on was that *he* would be there.

Seeing him was like crashing through thin ice. The moment came and quickly went. I put on my happy face and gave him a hug. Then I excused myself and ran into the woods to cry my eyes out.

I deal with bitter memories by covering them up and building walls. Admittedly, this is not a great practice. However, when it's unlikely that you'll face your problem, it's the easiest way to sweep the pain under the rug. I couldn't hide this time though; his love had touched me deeply, and here it surfaced in full force.

The time together was difficult, figuring out how to handle each other's presence. It was painfully apparent, though, that there was no going back. It must have been our efforts to keep our love that transformed us into new people. I guess that's when you know it's not for good, when you know the relationship is just a stepping stone for some bigger plan. Someday I'll understand why we weren't meant for each other.

What a faith journey this road I've traveled has been. I turned to my faith when it all began. I prayed to God to let me be open to this new relationship and the possibility of love. In return, I was presented with exactly that. It *was* overwhelming, but it was so perfect.

When I was struggling with the break-up, I wondered where God was. Why couldn't I just forget and move on?

I later realized that I struggled for a reason. I needed to learn what real love looks like, feels like, acts like. I had to learn that true love really exists but comes at a price. God put us together one year later purposefully. Being faced with each other forced us to open our eyes to the reality of what had become. No more pretending . . . this was real life and this was who we'd become.

Picking up the pieces would have been the easy solution. However, it would have opened up the same old can of worms and we both would have been hurt worse than before. Instead,

God did it so that we could see how far we'd come in all of our anguish. Otherwise, we might have gone on wondering forever.

Christine Brauer, Montana–Northern Wyoming Conference

JAMBO, RAFIKI

I'm a child of church camp—specifically Dunkirk Conference Grounds in Western New York. I couldn't wait to attend when I was ten years old, and I stayed involved there every summer until I graduated from high school. It was at camp that I first began to understand that perhaps not every story in the Bible was intended to be taken literally. It was at camp that I learned that other adults besides my parents could help me to learn what it means to be a Christian. God touched me through the people I met.

I remember that in my early years at camp, we had missionaries from abroad come and visit and spend time with us. A man named Peter, who came from Kenya, taught me how to say "Jambo, rafiki!" [Hello, friend!] in Swahili. Many of the things I learned at camp, I've never forgotten.

When I got into high school, I couldn't wait to be a volunteer at camp. In those days, youth could volunteer to be waitresses for family camp. Now, all these years later, I am still in touch with the person who was my head waitress, and I value her friendship and the guidance she gave me. Another friend, who was on the grounds crew, invited me to visit his college, and that's where I ended up going for my first two years.

Fifteen years after I graduated from high school, I returned to Dunkirk Conference Grounds to be a volunteer camp director for Junior High Camp. I wanted to give something back to the place that had nurtured me in my faith! By the way, I used counselors who had just graduated from high school themselves, and found them to be a very responsible group, who were willing to share their own faith stories with junior high kids. It reminds me of that great camp song that is so real, "You want to pass it on!"

Marja L. Coons-Torn, Pennsylvania Central Conference

SACRED SPACE

It was my first time at Silver Lake Conference Center. I was in seventh grade and had been encouraged by my sister to go for a week of camp. I can still remember packing my foot locker full of clothes complete with my name tag sewn into the shirts just in case I lost one—compliments of my mother. First impressions are important for a seventh grader. I only remember one thing about that week but it was a critical remembrance that to this day impacts my understanding of God.

For the first time in my life I worshiped outdoors. We would worship each morning in Hubbell Chapel, a beautiful outdoor chapel that overlooked the lake from on high. I remember the first time I entered this sacred space and thought to myself, *Now, this place is a lot different than the stained glass sanctuary I've worshiped in up to this moment.* My eyes were drawn skyward amidst those tall pine trees and I thought, *Surely God is in this sacred place!* Everything about worship seemed different now because of that space: the hymns were sung differently, the Scriptures seemed to come alive, the prayers seemed more real to me for unexplained reasons. I would return to that chapel year after year and be reminded anew about my first glimpse of the Holy One's presence in worship.

Kent J. Siladi, Florida Conference

HEAR THE CALL

Summer church camp and Boy Scout camp were essential summer experiences when I grew up. At church camp one memorable summer we were treated to the fabulous singing of a young seminarian. He was enthusiastic and truly alive in his commitment to becoming ordained and unashamed of using the gifts of his voice to glorify God. Around vesper camp fires and in the assembly hall, we all wanted to be near Johnny. His vibrant personality and energy were contagious. He represented all that is good and wonderful, vital and relevant about the church.

When I went to college, I met other students who had been at that same camp. There were some who had attended other camps where I had been as well. We just hadn't known we were headed for the same campus. Early in that first year, I didn't know what I wanted to do with my life. Today I know that my decision was influenced in large part by the conspicuous number of those former church campers who committed themselves to Christian vocations, including ordained ministry. Today I believe my call to ministry came—at least in part—from God through them. God was speaking through those youth with whom I shared camp fires, morning watch, and cabin shenanigans. God touched my life through dedicated counselors and directors, seminary interns like Johnny, and overseas guests who came to church camp for a week and introduced us to the joy and challenge of Christian service.

God spoke in those sacred settings through those special persons. God still touches us that way—in the lives and witness of the women and men, youth and children who are God's great church universal.

John Gantt, Central Pacific Conference

STILLING THE STORM

Llegó por fin los días que tanto habíamos esperado. Un grupo de treinta y cuatro jóvenes estábamos al punto de encontrarnos para celebrar un taller de liderazgo espiritual. El lugar seleccionado fue un campo cerca de la cuidad de Bayamo. Las características del taller requerian un lugar donde hubiera espacio para algunos juegos que formaban parte de la dinámica de grupo. Pero habia algo que como coordinador de taller me preocupaba. Estábamos en primavera y la lluvia podía ser un obstáculo para la realización del taller a tal punto que si llovía tendríamos que suspender la actividad.

Cuando ya estabamos todos los participantes listos para comenzar nuestra primera tarde de taller el cielo comenzó a ponerse muy oscuro y una fuerte lluvia nos amenazaba con intenciones de caer.

Desde el punto de vista humano, aquella lluvia era imposible que no cayera y nos impidiera la celebración del taller, pero tres hermanos nos tomamos de la mano y comenzamos a orar y pedirle a Dios que detuviera la lluvia.

Fue un verdadero milagro. El aire comenzó a soplar y se llevó hacia otros rumbos la tormenta que nos amenazaba.

Felizmente tuvimos tres dias de taller sin las amenazas del tiempo y todos podimos, juntos experimentar que "Dios tiene control de la naturaleza."

At long last the days we had been so eagerly awaiting had arrived. A group of thirty-four youth were about to meet for a spiritual leadership workshop. The site we had chosen was in the countryside near the city of Bayamo. The characteristics of the workshop required a location where there would be plenty of space for some games that would create part of the group dynamics. But there was something that, as the coordinator of the workshop, had me worried. It was spring and the rain could be an obstacle to the success of the workshop since, if it rained, we would have to suspend the activity.

When all of the participants were ready to begin on our first afternoon of the workshop the sky began to turn very dark and a strong rain storm threatened.

From the human point of view it was impossible that that rain not fall and impede the workshop, but three brothers took us by the hand and we began to pray and to beg God to stop the rain.

It was a true miracle. The wind began to blow and the storm that had threatened us was carried elsewhere.

Happily, we had three days of the workshop with no threats of bad weather and we could all experience together that "God has control of nature."

Ayan Zamora Guilarte, Pentecostal Christian Church of Cuba

Translation, Ellen H. Fries

3

FOR ALL THE SAINTS

A HERO IS A GIFT

Kevin was a good friend. We met during my sophomore year in high school. Up to that point, I didn't have any friends, so I was happy to have him as a companion, even if he was a year older. We had lunch together every day until his sudden and unexpected departure from school two years later. I went on to become a senior, puzzled about what happened to my friend.

During freshman year at the University of Hawai'i, I learned some terrible news. Kevin was killed by a car bomb while serving in the U.S. military in Baghdad. I stood staring at the newspaper, utterly horrified. Kevin was one of the only true friends I ever had. Although I did not show much on the outside, I felt completely devastated.

The news of Kevin's death frightened me into thinking I'd always be alone. I'm not a person who tends to cry a lot. In times of great stress or tragedy, I hold all of my feelings inside me. It's one of the worst feelings in the world. With Kevin's death, I became even more stressed about my life and what the future holds.

But as I carried on through this painful ordeal, I came to realize that I had much to be thankful for. Kevin had been there for me when I needed him. His loyalty to me was incomparable by any measure. Although I will never see him again, I can now remember him for his heroic qualities and willingness to spend time with me during those lonely years. There is little doubt in my mind that Kevin was a gift from God. With this new realization, I live more peacefully knowing that I've been truly blessed.

Prayer: Dear God, thank you for blessing me with friends like Kevin. I see lives like his as a sign of your awesome love for me. Keep me faithful in my walk with you, for I know that you alone are my strength. In Christ's name I pray. Amen.

Matthew Leong, Hawai'i Conference

THE ESSENTIAL ELEMENTS

You'd probably never expect a chemistry professor to be someone who'd take an interest in your spiritual growth, but that's how it was for me.

Dr. John Senne was in his first year of teaching during my first year in college. I can't remember exactly how our relationship began to be more than just teacher and student, but eventually that's how it grew. Dr. Senne was more genuine and transparent than anyone I knew. It probably sounds crazy, but when I learned that each afternoon he was confident and humble enough to post a sign on his office door saying "Please don't disturb—I'm napping" I knew this was someone unlike most adults I knew.

Eventually our relationship grew to the point where I was invited to his home for once-a-week Bible studies and on many mornings I met him in his office for Bible reading and prayer. He was a superb teacher (it's not his fault I'm a pastor today and not a chemist!), and a wicked table tennis player (we must have played hundreds of times during my four years in school and I never beat him. Not once!). He had an infectious laugh, and his care for my fellow students and me along with his transparent approach to life taught volumes about what it means to be a Christian. A big part of my growth in faith was encouraged and cultivated by John Senne and I will always be grateful for his friendship and the way God touched me through him.

Rich Pleva, Iowa Conference

A TRUE FRIEND IS CLOSER THAN YOUR OWN FAMILY

As I have been a member of the First Congregational Church UCC of Houston all my life, the members there have been more to me than friends—we are a family. Few people know me as well as that faithful community at FCC who have helped to raise me into the person I am today.

One friend in particular has been not only a supportive figure in my life, but a true inspiration for how I live my life and what I strive to be. "Mama Shirley," a fellow choir member of mine, has been there for me since my infancy, holding me, playing with me, teaching me to walk and talk. When I joined the church's adult choir, Shirley immediately offered to drive me to and from practice every Thursday night. It was during these long car rides that Shirley and I had the most interesting conversations and shared the secrets of our lives. She gave me advice for the sticky situations that I found myself in and showed me what it takes to be a good friend and a good Christian.

Not only does Shirley show her friendship through listening and talking with me but through her simple but meaningful actions. When I almost passed out in choir one evening, it was Shirley who immediately began to care for me, throwing orders at me to sit down, drink water, and eat something. I admire her youthful energy, positive outlook on life, and the amazing power her smile holds.

Now, as the summer intern (Summer Adult Laity Training, or SALT worker) at FCC, I feel privileged to have the opportunity to work with all of the supportive friends who played such a huge role in raising me. I have enjoyed spending this summer before I leave for college working with those who inspire me most. Through teaching a Sunday school class, I try to continue the tradition of teaching our church's children to be loving people and show God's love through their friendship to one another. It is through these children that I have a chance to spread God's love for generations to come.

Tricia Earl, South Central Conference

THE SEEDLING AND THE SHOVEL

Being a grandparent myself, I like to remember my grandparents and the joy of being in their presence. As a child I was blessed to know three of my grandparents well. My mother's mother died before I was born so I never knew her, though I heard many stories about her. My mother's father lived in a town some distance from the town I lived in. Sometimes we would take the train to visit him; at other times we went by car. I cherish those visits and have clear pictures of grandfather and his Irish setter, Pat. I could write a book about him but this essay is about my father's father.

My father's parents lived only a few blocks from our house. Some of my earliest memories are of visiting my grandfather's clothing store and seeing him reading his Danish newspaper. In my childhood and youth I spent many summers with my grandfather and grandmother. Our family had a summer cottage next to theirs. My brother and sisters and I and our mother would spend the summer months at the lake. My father would commute on the weekends. Even to this day I can hear my grandfather tell me, "There is a place for everything and everything has its place." His world was orderly and neat.

One of my fondest memories comes from the summer my grandfather, my brother, and I planted trees in the open field across the road from our cottage. I have no idea how many trees we planted that summer but it must have been a forest, or so it seems. My brother and I would walk to the field. One of us carried the bucket of small trees, the other a bucket of water. We both carried shovels. We'd spend the afternoon breaking open the soil, pouring in the water, planting the seedling, closing the hole, and pouring more water and moving on to plant the next tree. I remember asking my grandfather why we were planting so many trees. His answer was always the same. He would tell me, "There will be future generations that come here and they will enjoy these trees." I loved that idea. Future generations would enjoy the trees my brother and I were planting with our grandfather.

My grandfather helped me learn that even as a child I had both the opportunity and the responsibility to contribute to the beauty of the world for the sake of future generations that I will never know. It was one of the greatest lessons of my life.

David Hansen, Kansas-Oklahoma Conference

LETTING GO

In 1994, a new pastor came to my church. He seemed like a nice guy, and his sermons held my attention. Rev. Jeffery Whitman spent a little more than ten years at Colonial Park United Church of Christ in Harrisburg, Pennsylvania, and every moment I spent with him, I knew that I was with a good person. God spoke to all the youth at CPUCC through Jeff. He helped us learn to know and love God at our own level. He explained to us that God loved us no matter what and we should be happy with who we were, no matter what. We took trips to our church camp in the winter and around the Northeast in the spring. We had so much fun, and we learned about God the whole time.

Jeff left CPUCC to become our area conference minister. I was devastated when I heard he was leaving. Later that evening, I went to Jeff's house to talk to him about it. He told me that this was the direction that God was pointing him and that it was not that he was unhappy at CPUCC—God just wanted him to move on. That made it okay for me. I knew that God needed Jeff elsewhere, and I had to accept that whether I liked it or not. He still was the counselor at the church camp's Music and Drama Camp, which I attended every year. He also spoke to me a lot about going into the ministry. I never really felt called and am currently at Penn State University studying mechanical engineering, but I am glad that he saw something in me and thought that I had potential. Because of Jeff's influence now and then, I will always feel that I need to be involved in the church. The church is a part of me, and he helped make it that way.

This year, Jeff called me one night to say he was the candidate for a conference minister position in Missouri. I was upset, but I remembered what he said to me when he left CPUCC. It was time for God to use Jeff to help other people. I know that I will not get to see him often, but I know that Rev. Jeff Whitman has helped me become the person I am today through his actions and words.

Bryan C. Fischer, Pennsylvania Central Conference

SAINT WITH A CROOKED CROWN

Many adults look at their experience in traditional Sunday school, and special teachers (God bless those saints of the church!) stand out. I still carry memories of several such people and give thanks for what I learned from them. But in junior high, I experienced a very different kind of teacher. His name was Tom, and he was a senior in high school.

There was nothing traditional about Tom—not in what he taught, how he dressed, or how he acted. He had a reputation as a bit of a rebel (no certain cause), and he dressed in what one might describe as the fashion of the beatniks. I remember being shocked that he even *came* to church, so to have him be presented as my Sunday school teacher was even more shocking. Our class was small—just a handful of boys—and perhaps whoever recruited Tom realized that a different kind of teacher was needed to make an impression on us. And perhaps that same recruiter thought that the experience of teaching junior high boys might shape Tom in positive, new ways.

I don't remember classes in detail, but I do remember with great clarity several particular occasions. One was when Tom bribed the class with an offer to buy a milkshake at the local soda fountain for anyone who came the next Sunday able to recite the Ten Commandments. His intent was that we simply have the list of ten in mind, but when I looked up Exodus 20, I thought he must have meant for us to memorize verses 1–17— a much more demanding task. I dutifully did so, and when I recited all of those verses on the next Sunday, Tom's jaw dropped in surprise. When I finished, he announced with glee that I had earned two milkshakes for that!

Another fond memory I carry is of a Saturday outing Tom engineered for our class. We all hopped in his car and drove into the nearby mountains (not an outing that would conform with today's Safe Church practices!). We found a great slope that was covered with deep snow with a hard crust and few trees, and we proceeded to spend hours skiing down that slope on the soles of our shoes.

In the course of that year, a special friendship formed between Tom and us, so one day when he came to the Sunday morning class with an obvious black eye, he found a way to divert our attention without going into detail about whatever adventure he'd had the night before that led to it—clearly it was not something he wanted to admit to his Sunday school class!

I recently ran into Tom after the passing of some fifty years. I reminded him that he had been my teacher for a year, and while he seemed surprised that I felt I had learned anything from him, he was clearly pleased to know that he had made a memorable impression on my life.

Randall Hyvonen, Montana–Northern Wyoming Conference

A PERSONAL GPS

I have not really had the experience in my life where my faith was completely turned around. There was no moment where I woke up one morning and the clouds parted and the sun shined through my window and God said, "EMILY, I AM CALLING YOU!" Actually, God came to me in a more subtle and quiet way. It was so subtle that I didn't even notice it had happened until after it had already happened. God sent Wiebke Waltersdorf into my life.

From about seventh grade to freshman year in high school, I had gone to numerous retreats that our church had to offer. But because I was so shy, I barely got the same effect out of them as all the others who went to them did. I was always scared to share my ideas and get involved because I didn't think anyone would listen to me.

One day after church, during my sophomore year, Wiebke came up to me and asked me if I wanted to help lead a retreat for middle schoolers. I was really hesitant, because there would be no one else there that I knew, so that really scared me. But Wiebke kept pushing me, and soon she had basically signed me up without me really saying yes. That was Wiebke though; she pushed people. Sometimes, as I look back, I remember that I really did not like it when she would just sign me up for something, but now I am really glad that she made me try something new.

When Wiebke pushed me to try something new, I don't know if she realized that it changed me a lot. It got me involved when I was too shy to get involved before. She aided me in finding my own faith and how I wanted to express my faith to God.

So, it wasn't really God saying to me, "EMILY GET INVOLVED WITH YOUTH MINISTRY!" God had Wiebke and I cross paths, and now I am no longer afraid to just jump in and try something.

Emily Bass, Wisconsin Conference

LIKE JOSEPH

Every Christmas when I looked at the figures around the manger, I felt closest to Joseph. Probably he reminded me of my father: not much of a talker, not a scene-grabber, solidly providing shelter and sustenance, sent by God.

My father had maybe completed second grade. He lived and died within a half-mile stretch of sandy soil; grew up speaking German and married a woman who grew up speaking some archaic Slovak dialect; and brought home the newspaper like a daily badge of honor, ready to read the obituaries and the crop prices. His huge hands repaired the Farmall tractor like a family friend, shoveled manure and molten steel, and lifted babies tenderly and securely to the skies.

How does such a man show what he feels except by getting up at 4:00 A.M. to ride to the factory and work until 3:00 P.M., taking the overtime whenever it came his way; and coming home to work the farm; and, oh yes, hacking a lawn from the weeds, and cleaning the septic tank, and patching the roof, putting up the warping storm windows every November, and keeping tar and paint close at hand for every occasion, and giving you a house to grow up in?

It was never a grand house, or a convenient house. On good days it came close to "cozy."

It was always small. Confining. Not set up for panoramic views or cross ventilation. No room for a desk to do homework or a private place to score the libretto of the soul.

My father offered this house as his expression of care, more delicate than any of my gulping syllables. No wonder that every Christmas I felt close to Joseph, who had resolutely found a safe place for Jesus to be born. Both gave love that endures, and sees you through whatever may assail you.

Mary Susan Gast, California, Nevada Northern Conference

SARGE

I was eight years old when I had an "experience with God" that left me without any question that my future vocation was to be as an ordained Christian minister. It happened on Parker Road as I was making my way home from school on an October weekday. The spot is still there. I have been back to visit it many times since. But what occurred there was a once-in-a-lifetime experience. It left me with feelings of both awe and complete terror.

There was only one person in whom I could confide. She was the director of Christian education at our church. Her given name was Margaret, but we called her "Sarge." She ran a Sunday school program with more than three hundred children and she had a voice that could penetrate twelve inches of concrete and make a teenage boy stop dead in his tracks. But she also cared for all of us. I knew I could tell her what happened and she would understand.

Throughout my teenage years Sarge quietly and gently encouraged me. Her encouragement was extremely important. It was the Vietnam years and my generation was increasingly estranged from the institutional church. It took courage to admit that you were actually planning to become a minister. Sarge was present at my Ecclesiastical Council and ordination and has kept in touch with me at each step in my ministry. It really is true what has been said about Christianity: "It's not about the rules; it's about relationships!"

Stephen Gray, Indiana-Kentucky Conference

A REFLECTION OF GOD

Annie was someone who influenced me in a positive way and nurtured me in my faith. She lived across the street from me, across from the house I moved into when I was seven, and we became fast friends. It hardly mattered that she was older than my grandparents and many times my age—I connected with her because she made me feel comfortable. She affirmed me for who I was, and she always treated me with kindness and respect.

Over the years, Annie got to know me very well. I confided in her and knew that she understood me in a unique way. Annie also knew my family well, so I know that she was aware that we were not religious. I do not recall who brought up God first, but I remember the conversation—the feeling of anticipation, the light in the front room of her home. Annie offered me a book by a famous preacher and evangelist, and I remember thinking that if Annie thought I might get something from it, that I would give it a try. I deeply loved and respected her, as a role model and a guide in my life. . . . I was willing to follow her guidance in faith too.

When I think of that day, and the step that Annie helped me take, I am reminded of a core principle of my work: you have to have a relationship with a young person to be able to talk about God. Matters of faith are deeply important, and often they are also very personal and sensitive. I responded to Annie's nudging toward God because she had earned the right to approach me, and it became one of the first positive steps I took toward a personal relationship with God. This kind, elderly neighbor introduced me to the God of the universe, who, like her, knew me by name and loved me as I am.

God spoke to me through Annie, and now I work in youth ministry because I hope that in some way God can speak through me to the young people I serve. That hope is the source of a lot of personal pressure, but it also reminds me what an incredible privilege, and responsibility, I have with the work I do. In my ministry I still see God most clearly through people— through the young people I work with; through my husband, family, and friends; through the clergy of my church; through the people I am blessed to serve in missions; and through the stories of people I will never meet.

Hilary Flynn, Minnesota Conference

WALKING IN THE PRESENCE OF GOD

Walking into Panera Bread in Owasso, Oklahoma, tonight, I was in search of a latte and WiFi. The ice storm hit here Sunday. It's Wednesday and utilities are still off save for this oasis. A doctor sits behind me calling patients and sending e-mail prescriptions to the pharmacy. A tutor is helping two college students prepare for their calculus finals. Families from this neighborhood greet each other and say they are blessed. God's presence is here.

Earlier today, I drove by the Community of Hope United Church of Christ in Tulsa, where the utilities are off and two old trees lost their tops and the limbs filled the parking lot. Inside, the warmth of Sundays past filled me although the building was cold and dark. God's presence was there.

I learned to walk in the presence of God as a young child. My parents showed me the way. We were farmer/ranchers where one was totally dependent on the elements of nature, which we ascribed to God's realm. So it was that my parents said they trusted God in good times and dire times. It's true. They did and I do.

On our 160-acre farm, allotted under the Dawes Commission of the Federal Government to us as Muscogee (Creek) people in Oklahoma, one walked in the presence of God. My parents acknowledge God's morning light and God's setting sun with prayers and conversation. It was a way of life and that way of life has become mine.

Thank you, God, for allowing humans and all of creation to be and to walk in your presence. Amen.

Rosemary McCombs Maxey, Council for American Indian Ministry

4   BLESSINGS FOR THE EDGES OF LIFE

GOING AWAY TO COME HOME

Sitting in the stiff, cold pew, I bent my head in an attempt to hide my tears. It was not easy for me to be in a church because of all the things I had experienced at my "home church" the previous two years. Being there at that little church in Germany, thousands of miles away from the pews I sat in nearly every Sunday for thirteen years, brought back painful memories I wished I could erase, yet at the same time, there was no other place in the world I would rather have been.

Finally, the Young Ambassadors were together again. The Indiana-Kentucky Conference established an exchange program for youth with the Evangelical Church of Westphalia, Germany, and I was blessed to be a part of it. Never would I have thought such a program would impact my life in such a dramatic way. As I struggled with losing my home church, I had my American and German sisters and brothers in Christ to help me through my difficult times of uncertainty and change.

My tears flowed that evening not only because it was the last night of the program and I would be returning home the next morning but because I knew I was truly experiencing the church—the body of Christ. At that moment I was filled with hope and vision for what the church really could be. At that moment I was surrounded by a love I pray all may one day feel. At that moment I felt God.

As my beloved friends embraced me, wiping my tears away, I felt the embrace of God in a stunning mountaintop experience, and I was filled with awe and terror at the thought of coming down from that sacred place. I would have to face the world once again, but I knew with a renewed sense of hope that God would always be guiding me to fulfill the call given to me.

Sarah Frische-Mouri, Indiana-Kentucky Conference

SHARE WHAT WE HAVE OR TAKE WHAT WE WANT . . .

In conversation with my wife Patricia, she mentioned that her eighth grade classroom, wonderfully smart students, had a discussion about how we share what we have and how some in history take what they want. Patricia's class was excited to converse about the historic scenario that seems to repeat itself, over and over again in America. When this nation was formed, the "explorers" and "settlers" found a generous and self-determining Indian people. It was as if the settlers began by taking residence in the Indian's house or home while never really being invited in. They entered in forceful ways in most cases. It was as though the intruders were demanding a bedroom and exclusive use of a bathroom, unrestricted use of the kitchen, closet space, and a space in the garage to park their car. The host and homeowner, the Indians, could not say a word, found few ways to object, or do anything. The image was vivid for the students. For their trouble, this host gained alcoholism, disease, and a fractured community. The question Patricia asked her class was, "How would you feel?"

Growing up black in America was difficult for me, with constant infringement and intrusion by those who took great advantage of their privilege. The school system I attended, particularly in high school, was multiracial but the curriculum was heavily slanted. Learning about significant accomplishments of Africans and African Americans was largely nonexistent. It was in the Faith Congregational Church in Hartford, Connecticut, that I learned something about my own history and the historic journey and heritage of the African American people. It was there that I learned that the *Amistad* sailed and that black people contributed greatly to the shaping and growth of America. Jesus was not some benevolent white man for me and never was he one who condoned injustice, but rather Jesus and justice were hand and hand, strong and sure. Jesus led my way early and deeply in my life—still does to this day.

So it was that I would learn to speak truth to power, to live life unprotective of my job or career, but seeking to stand up for the least, the left out, and the lost around me. Through my early experiences, I learned that my faith guides and informs, that it is not about privilege but willingness to speak the truth, living as truthfully as possible, knowing that it is good to share what we have, rather than living life seeking to take what we want. When I learned that faith lesson, life was and is better.

Stephen W. Camp, Southern Conference

A BIGGER FAMILY

Thanksgiving has never been an especially exciting holiday for me. I've never really liked turkey, and only a few years ago did I brave the cranberry sauce. Not to mention that last year was my first turkey day as a vegetarian—so my big meals consist mostly of mashed potatoes and mac and cheese.

But this year will be different. This year, I'm having two Thanksgiving dinners. Twice the starch, twice the fun, right? Well, yes, but that's not why I'm excited.

On Thanksgiving day, I will be celebrating with my family, as usual. But on the Tuesday before, I'll be at a friend's house all dressed up with thirty other kids from my high school, because we thought it would be fun to have a sit-down meal together outside of the cafeteria.

But what is so special about this gathering is not something you'll be able to see on the surface. What is special is who we are, and what brings us to the table together. We are really very different people.

Though we all come from Christ-based beginnings, we've all ended up being very diverse, religiously. Two of us are Catholics, one devout, one doubting. Several are conservative Christians, very dedicated. Quite a few are more liberal Christians, some liberal in their belief in Christ, others certain, but open to other religions. One has dabbled in Buddhism, some look at Hinduism, many of us meditate. One decided very recently that she is an atheist, and a few would identify with agnosticism.

While many of the invited are heterosexual, a few are not. Many are peacemongers, but some still support the war. Some make sure to recycle, some try to use less gas, some don't notice that kind of thing.

These qualities are important these days. Important in uniting people, they have also begun to tear us apart. The hatred on both sides of these debates makes me so sad—the friendships that are completely destroyed, the families that don't stick together.

But that's where Thanksgiving comes in, and God, if that's the name you choose. When I look around that table this fall and see everyone's faces lit up, when I realize again that the debate that tears us apart is not the most important thing in the world—that fellowship is—that's when I'll give thanks. Because we have so much to be thankful for.

Jennie Wachowski, Kansas-Oklahoma Conference

SONGS OF THE SPIRIT

When I was seventeen, my grandfather and father died, both un-expectedly, just two weeks apart. My father was my pulse, my grandfather my pastor. Each were powerful figures in my life as their word was often the last, if not the only, to be considered. At their deaths, I felt rudderless, confused, and alone. It was my senior year in high school. Plans for my future had to be put on hold.

While my faith had always provided me strength and direc-tion, it did not feel strong enough for what I needed in those days. This enormous, unsettling loss rocked me to the core. I did not question God's existence, but neither did I feel access to God's presence and grace. This was an unfamiliar reality for me. Until the moment of my father and grandfather's deaths, I knew with each breath God's presence in my life, in every life. I needed something to fill the void. Familiar words from scripture were helpful, but not enough.

As time went by, I often found myself humming hymns we sang in worship or singing silly songs we learned in Sunday school. At the center of my being, I could hear people sing spir-ituals and anthems as if especially for me. There was never a specific song, nor was there a specific voice. Instead, there were a variety of (godly/divine) voices offering a melody of hope and healing to my broken heart.

Through the music of my faith, I began to feel God's pres-ence. When humming or singing, I felt God's embrace. Words, melody, and rhythm opened my heart to God's healing grace. Plans for my future were made.

To this day, whenever life takes an unexpected turn, it is the music of my faith that puts me back on center. In the melody, I always find God's healing grace.

Susan A. Henderson, Vermont Conference

GIDEON

Though I haven't really been the type of person to compare my-self to anyone or any story that I read about in the Bible, lately, I have taken an interest in the story of Gideon in the seventh chapter of Judges, where Gideon is preparing to go to battle with the Midianites. Twice before he is set to go to battle, God tells Gideon that he has too many men in his army, and that he must let some of them go so that the people will know that it was because of God that Gideon will win the battle.

At some point, Gideon made the decision to give himself and his men up to God and God's will. Yet I feel that it wasn't necessarily the stereotypical resignation of absolute, unshakable faith, but rather the feeling of there is nothing else to do now, so I might as well just do what God says. I feel that when this story is viewed as yet another of the scriptures about our struggles, ending with people faithfully putting their trust in God, it is not being seen completely.

You see, being born to a drug-addicted, teenaged mother who couldn't have cared less about me, and bouncing around from friend's house to friend's house for more than a year, until being taken in by my godmother, who would later adopt me, I like to think that it was ME that pulled through, that I am the master of my own fate in the sense that I am the only one responsible for who I am today, and that God played a cameo role in it all. But the truth is, without God, things would have been very different for me. So to me, Gideon reaches that point only at the very end, and only because of the absolute proof provided by God. Before reaching such a point, Gideon felt more like he had no other choice: he had dismissed nearly his entire army, so there really was nothing he could do except listen to God or go home. But when God showed Gideon the plans of the enemy, this was the crucial point where Gideon went from apathetic resignation to genuine faith and trust, if not complete understanding.

Gideon spends most of this story struggling to accept what God tells him to do, especially the specific reasoning why. Often times, we as human beings find it impossible to understand the ways of God, God's reasons for some of the things that happen. We are not God's confidants, for God is all-knowing. But because God is all-knowing, as well as all-loving, God understands our fears and doubts, our apprehensions about giving ourselves to faith in God. God forgives us for whatever it is we may do and possesses infinite patience with our trouble in accepting God's ways. It is not so much that God lays out our lives for us beforehand, but rather that God sets down the paths for us to walk, with signs suggesting the better paths to travel. No matter how big or obvious the signs may be, we will find ways to stumble onto the harder paths from time to time, yet God is always waiting to take our hand and guide us back to let us choose another path.

John Allen, Florida Conference

WAKE-UP CALL

As a teenager, I experienced God as a stern force of holiness and judgment. The Holiness/Pentecostal churches in which I was raised did not fail to admonish me about the fact that if I did not live up to the high and holy standards of God's righteousness, I would surely face God's eternal wrath. Holiness meant living a life of complete personal piety, with no carnal indulgence to separate my soul from my Savior. Holiness meant refusing to yield to the worldly lusts of the flesh—which were primarily fornication (any sex outside of marriage); listening to and dancing to music that inspired lust (that is, secular music); taking drugs (for instance, smoking pot) and disrespecting authority (being disobedient to parents and pastor). Deeply entrenched in the sermons I listened to while I was a teen were the words: "Come out from among them (people of the world) and be ye separate, says the Lord your God." And I'll never forget this: "Holiness is not going to come down to you. You've got to come up to holiness!"

In other words, God's standard of righteousness would never condescend to accommodate my sinfulness.

At the age of about fourteen, however, something happened that shook my understanding of God's holiness and the church's righteousness. A bright, brilliant, beautiful teenage male, two years my senior, was constantly berated, mocked, and scorned by members of my church and by me for being a "faggot." The denunciations and derogatory comments toward this young man were fairly commonplace and were blatantly expressed on a daily basis. I myself felt justified in parroting these insults because they were espoused and sanctioned by the preachments and teachings of the church I attended—the arbiter of divine holiness.

I thought little about the personal and psychological impact that our words of judgment and sentiments of rejection had upon this young man. It was simply the way things were, and more importantly, the way God had ordained things to be. This young man wouldn't attend church, which only seemed to verify his imminent damnation.

In a one-on-one conversation with him one day, he made the statement: "Nobody loves me." "God loves everybody who repents," I said. He just looked at me. Approximately one week later, he was dead.

Not many details about his death were forthcoming. Was it a murderous hate crime or a desperate suicide? I may never know. I do remember being in the company of some fellow church members when his death was announced. They shook their heads in disbelief, and expressed their grief in tears. But in my heart I knew that there was something deeply wrong with this sanctimonious show of sorrow. The fact that we could righteously express sadness at his death, and yet give him no encouragement to live as God made him did not sit well with me. I had no theological capacity to challenge what had happened, but in my heart of hearts I knew it wasn't right. Somehow I knew that the church's caustic homophobia draped in myopic holiness was the real killer.

Kenneth L. Samuel, Southeast Conference

A BLESSING ON THE EDGE

After spending a week and a half in rural Zimbabwe, I was shocked to stand before an immense display of God's power and beauty at Victoria Falls. I was on a mission trip in the summer of 2007, and we had recently finished a week of work at Africa University in Old Mutare, Zimbabwe. During our time at the university we had maintained our dedication to our mission by helping the school and connecting with the people we met. We interacted with people from all walks of life including students from the far reaches of the African continent, farm workers from the University Farm, and the happy children who called the local orphanage home.

I went from this down-to-earth, amazingly generous environment, to standing on the edge of a cliff overlooking the long stretch of falls that compose one of the Seven Natural Wonders of the World. I had moved from the great poverty of God's rural people to the great wealth of God's power as contained in the falls. The contrast was not the only thing to stand out in the new environment. There was also a different interest in the falls on behalf of the visitors, an interest that did not exist in respect to the rural poor. God was present in each situation, but it seemed that people's attention was more focused on the falls, a touristy destination where spending money on souvenirs was easier than volunteering time for a cause.

The area around Victoria Falls is flat with a level plain of trees stretching for miles. The only change on the plain is a great cloud that hangs over the falls. This cloud is the creation of mist from the thundering falls. It falls with such a force that visitors get soaked to the bone when walking along the edge. The falls are power condensed into a singular natural beauty that only stands to enhance the scenery around it.

The immense love of God was clear in the rural areas and at the falls. The power to love was just as great, and the desire to spread the love of God was never as strong as it was on my trip to Zimbabwe.

Meredith Jackson, California, Nevada Northern Conference

CONVERSION STORY

It was the year 1985. Probably many of you were not born yet. I was recently moved from my original country of Puerto Rico to the United States. By that time I was working as an office manager in a meat packing factory. The majority of our workers were undocumented. These workers were the only ones willing to work loading and unloading trucks in subzero temperatures during the winter and suffocating temperatures in the summer.

One afternoon, I was closing my accounting books when I heard screams coming from the main plant. They were saying, the *migra* is here! I had no idea what the *migra* was. One of the workers came running upstairs to alert me that the whole building was surrounded by the *migra*. When I looked out I saw several INS vehicles, then I understood that what the workers called the *migra*—the Immigration and Naturalization Service. They were knocking at the doors demanding to enter the premises because they received a call denouncing the factory as a place where undocumented workers were employed.

The workers, ten of them, were in total panic. I look around, and the only place where they could hide was the freezer. I told the workers to get into the freezer and I would lock the doors. They look at me in disbelief! Probably they thought that I was crazy by asking them to hide in a freezer, but the reality was that this was the only place that could accommodate all ten of them. So, they went into the freezer and I locked the door. Immediately, I opened the factory doors to allow the INS agents to enter. They were really rude, demanding to see the workers. I told them there was no one in the place, but me. They searched the entire place.

They were about to leave, when suddenly one of the agents noticed the freezer. He ordered me to open it. I was trembling, and for the first time in my life I prayed really hard. I must mention that I was a cultural Catholic, which is to say that you attend church on four occasions: baptisms, weddings, funerals, and on Holy Friday.

So I started praying with all my heart. I began a silent dialogue with God. I said, God if you really exist, please do not allow these agents to find these people. Please, God, blind this agent or make these workers invisible to his sight. The agent repeated his order for me to open the door. My hand was trembling, but I open the door and he entered the freezer. About two minutes later he came back saying there was no one in there.

I could not believe what I heard because I knew that there were ten people inside. When the INS agents left, the workers came out and told me that when the agent said that there was no one there he was looking directly at them.

What happened that day? Many people will say that a miracle happened. What was the miracle? Maybe that God blinded the agent? I don't know. Maybe that God moved his heart and he choose to ignore their presence? I don't know.

All I know is that from that day on, I learned that there was a God that really answers your prayers. All I know is that from that day on, I became an activist on behalf of the undocumented workers. All I know is that God called me into serving in the United Church of Christ for twenty-three years. All I know is that day was my conversion day.

Carmen Alicia Nebot, Council for Hispanic Ministries

THE WORD IN THE WORLD

God works in mysterious and wonderful ways. God appears in our lives when we least expect it and when we most need it. God has appeared to me in many times over the past few years, as I've grown and changed the most in my faith in this time. He has shown himself in beautiful settings, like among five thousand people together in the French countryside in the community of Taize. He has found me when I am concerning myself with others, especially with the justice work I do for orphans in Africa. But there is one place where I know God always goes when I come.

At Lancaster Theological Seminary, I see God at work every time I visit (which is often). He was there when I, a newly communed church member, ventured to my first Leadership Academy seeking for something to believe in. He was there when I returned for my first round of global travel with the same community. God was present when I came around for a third summer as a staff member to help me reach out to others who were at a stage that I was once at too.

Each time I return, God is there. God is in the people that I love and adore and God is in the people that I meet each time I go back. I see him especially in the community of staff with whom I am privileged to work, for they show me what true love and friendship looks like. God is in my life, in the people whom I know, in the places where I go, and in the things that I see. It is beautiful.

Alyssa Leister, Pennsylvania Southeast Conference

CUANDO SUCEDE LO INESPERICADO SIGO CONFIANDO EN TI SEÑOR (WHEN THE UNEXPECTED HAPPENS, I KEEP TRUSTING IN MY GOD)

Comenzaba el año 2007 y al panecer todo marchaba a la perfección. Festejamas Navidad y Año Nuevo y mi vida gozaba de paz y Felicidad. Dios me dejaba experimenter su gozoen mi hogar y en mi Corazon. Estando aún dormida el viernes 12 de enero en la manana una llamada telefónica interumpió en la tranquilidad de mi familia. Mi madre se encontraba en el Hospital gravemente enfermas. Confiando en el Señor viajé hasta allá para cuidar de ella, con la ajuda de mi hermano y otros familiars. La salud de mi mamá empeoró y los medicis no hallabar una respuesta a su estado crítico. A tan solo una semana de la ber sido hospitalizada, mi madre, de ltan solo cincuenta y uno años, falleció, dejandonos a todos con el corazón destrozado por su separación, aunque sabiamos que había partido con el Señor ali vida no estaba preparada para ese triste y doloroso acontecimiento que me aparaba de la companía y el amor de oni madre. Se puso a panebeo dentro de mí aquello que aprendí desde niña en el evangelio que para nosotros el morir es ganancia. Una lucha entre mi mente que pensaba: erauna persona tan joven, a quien tanto amo y necesito y como pudo suceder, porqúe a ella? Pero mi corazón, muy en lo produndo sabe y reconoce que en esta tierra solo andaimos de paso, pues como dice su palabra solo somos peregrinos y extranjeros.

Cuando nuestra fé se ponea poelba aunque se dezare nuestro cuerpo de tanta sufrir, es necesario agarrarse fuerte de la mano del Señor hasta poder decir. "Presigo a la meta."

Las lágrimas corren por mis ojos al escribir esta difícil experiencia que marcó mi vida de una manera transcendental, donde solo la paz de Dios me ha sustentado para que hoy pueda expresar con segunidad que aun en los momentos mas difíciles e inesperadis you confío en mi Dios.

The year 2007 seemed to begin with all going along perfectly. We celebrated Christmas and New Year and my life was filled with peace and joy. God let me experience God's joy in my home and in my heart. On the morning of January 12 I was still asleep when a phone call interrupted the tranquility of my family. My mother was in the hospital gravely ill. Trusting in God, I went there to care for her with the help of my brother and other family members. My mother's condition worsened and the doctors could find no reason for her critical condition. Only a week after being hospitalized my mother, only 51 years old, died, leaving us all broken hearted to be separated from her, even though we knew that she was with God.

My life was not prepared for the deeply sad and painful occurrence of being separated from the love and companionship of my mother. This put to the test that which I had learned in the gospel since I was little: that for us death is a gain. There began a battle between my mind—the thought that she was such a young person whom I loved so much and whom I need. How could this happen? And why her?—and my heart, where deep down inside I knew and recognized that we are only on this earth for a little while, for as the word of God says, we are only pilgrims and strangers.

When our faith is put to the test although it may be painful, although it may be sad, although our body may be rent from so much suffering, it is necessary to hang on hard to the hand of Jesus until it is possible to say, "I continue on to the goal."

The tears run from my eyes as I describe this difficult experience that marked my life in a transcendental manner, where only the peace of God has sustained me so that today I can express with confidence that even in the most difficult and unexpected moments I trust in my God.

Litsandra Rodriguez Hernandez, Pentecostal Christian Church of Cuba
Translation, Ellen Fries

AFTER DARKNESS

I shuffle my feet. Blind. Feeling my way through darkness I follow the sound of feet before me. The warm breeze brushing my face, my eyes strain. Dark on dark, the outline of objects form.

Feeling loose, flat, uneven rock beneath me, an oily black river forms to my left. Everything becomes slightly lighter, just enough to make out a vague outline of my friends' faces.

As we sit, silence embraces us with a light sense of emotion.

The rock is cool against my hand. A light, pure, sweet voice breaks the silence. As I stare at the black river, Megan's words saturate my thoughts.

Taking a small candle from Megan's hands, I hold it as though it would shatter with the slightest movement. I stare at the tangible treasure, the metaphor of my beginning.

A flicker licks the air only to be snuffed out. Frustration forms after several attempts at lighting the candles. The slight breeze is snuffing out our success.

After several more tries, the cold black silence is again broken by Megan's voice. Raising her face and eyes towards the black, infinite sky, her words gently glide into a pleading question, "A little help here, please?"

The breeze stops. My mind and heart race.

Is this just coincidence? It had to . . . it couldn't . . . but it . . . HOW!?

My candle is now lit, shining in the blackness. Hypnotized, I stare at the dancing flame, until a small scalding twinge in my finger yanks me back into reality. I look around, noticing my friends' faintly glowing faces. Everyone is calm yet anxious. Quiet, yet their eyes question out loud.

After a moment of silence, we set our candles down, join hands in prayer, and then lead into "Sanctuary." After we finish "Sanctuary," silence again emerges. Flames smothered, we begin heading back. I hesitate, looking at the black water. My head is spinning. What really happened? Megan's words cradled my thoughts, bringing an immense amount of comfort. Everything was like a dream . . . and then that breeze. That moment, that one questioning moment. It happened in slow motion. The whole night was like a fairy tale. Everything stood still, everything ceased to exist, everything seemed to revolve around us. The Prayer. The Scripture. The flames.

The flames, smothered. Smothered in front of our eyes, but still lit in our hearts. My flame was lit, my faith sparked. Was that nature, or was that God? It was the nature of my God. Whether it was coincidence or truth, the entire night became my beginning.

Sense became real. Living gained a deeper purpose. Believing became life.

Lying in my bed, eyes straining in the darkness, the light burned in my eyes. It was dark, but everything was so clear and bright. That small light, that small flame, that vast darkness was a shot to the head, heart, and soul. And as I awoke, I became something different. I felt as though I was immersed in a new world.

Everything became realistic. Although still imaginative, creative, and abstract, I now knew what reality was.

Elizabeth Becker, Iowa Conference

5   **THE CHURCH FAMILY**

GOD WAS THERE

Every year my home church has at least one Youth Sunday, when the youth take over worship from planning to execution. About seven years ago, when I was thirteen, my mom was the superintendent of church school. Two days before Youth Sunday the scheduled youth speaker cancelled on her. So she asked (try begged) me to speak.

On the night before, I agreed. It took me four hours to write two pages on the topic of love. Finally I went to bed, and upon waking up the next morning I was very nervous. This feeling of anxiety and bad nerves didn't go away until I stood up in the pulpit to preach.

Ironically, when tense feelings should have risen highest they subsided and I felt an inner peace as if I had been preaching my entire life. It wasn't until later on that I realized that this was nothing but the anointing of the Holy Spirit comforting and empowering me. I preached for about ten minutes, one of the shortest sermons ever preached in a black church, and to be sure my shortest.

I lifted up marital love, which has become a sticky topic, and then encouraged the congregation to "get hitched to the Holy Ghost," or reaffirm their vows to God. I received instant "talk back" even from my rather quiet congregation. This was more than human approval, but God's own way of letting me know that it was OK to continue; keep going, God said to me.

The most interesting part of my experience of God on that day is very much apparent when I look back over the sermon text now. God had been present even as I was writing the sermon the night before. God had influenced the words and phrases. And it was God who used me to unknowingly write a sermon that was inclusive of all marital relationships. You see, the first sentence is, "When the love between *two people* is so strong, they get married."

J. Alan Williams, United Black Christians

WHAT DID THEY EXPECT?

What did they expect? My parents took me to our UCC church for a worship service or program of some kind more than once a week for the first sixteen years of my life. Apparently something rubbed off because by sixteen I had developed a social conscience about injustice in the world. Sometimes my values clashed with those of my parents. We disagreed about the Vietnam war. We disagreed about a woman's right to choose. We disagreed about strategies to achieve civil rights. What did they expect? They took me to our UCC church!

I experience the presence of God in many ways and one of the strongest is God's presence in the midst of a struggle for justice. In the '60s the General Synod of the United Church of Christ encouraged churches to elect youth on every committee. I was active in our youth group and was nominated to serve on the congregation's Mission and Social Action Committee. It was a little intimidating being the only person there under the age of eighteen. But I got to know some adults who really believed that Christian faith motivated them to engage the world in both direct hands-on volunteering and in systemic change. They prayed about this at every meeting—not just the minister, but regular people prayed too. It was holy ground like nothing else I'd experienced yet. They taught me how to listen for God's presence in the struggles for justice and then how to organize and act on my beliefs. Eventually my parents supported my efforts, even when we disagreed. What did they expect? They took me to church!

I know God uses us to work for justice when we are tuned in to God's presence.

Jane Heckles, California, Nevada Southern Conference

NO MATTER WHO YOU ARE OR WHERE YOU COME FROM, YOU ARE WELCOME HERE

Any denomination with the courage to speak such bold words and the compassion to see their message through can play no small part in its members' lives. This simply worded expression conveys the idea of an all-inclusive welcome to an audience of everyone, including and especially minorities, the poor, the downtrodden, the oppressed, and all members of society that history and traditional organized religion have otherwise looked down on. The role of the United Church of Christ in the lives of its members is not quite so general; the significance of our beliefs and morals hold a unique significance for each individual. To the poverty-stricken, homeless, and unemployed, the church is an understanding ear with sympathy for economic misfortune. In the eyes of the oppressed citizens of third-world countries and those suffering under intolerant governments, we are a beacon of hope for freedom. For every ethnic minority group that has been snubbed by religious exclusivity, homosexuals labeled sinners by an intolerant society, and immigrants turned away by a hostile nation, we are a set of open arms ready to welcome anyone, regardless of race, gender, or sexual orientation. Even to those fortunate few who seem to want for nothing in life, the church provides comfort for burdens that are not so evident.

And for myself, a native-born middle-class adolescent girl with enough comforts to take for granted, raised closely in and around the church for sixteen years? To me, the church is all of that. Regardless of where my ability to empathize with people of less fortunate circumstances ends or begins, I find that the influence of the church heals, inspires, comforts, and offers me absolute acceptance in equal measure, and despite my own personal shortcomings. Rather than a place of condemnation, the UCC portrays itself as a throughway for God's own divine acceptance. In setting an example of unconditional welcome and abiding love, the doctrine of the United Church of Christ has served to shape my life within as well as outside of the church.

By nature, the United Church of Christ is a denomination that defies tradition, and it is only fitting that membership in a UCC congregation should teach such progressive views as infinite compassion and extravagant welcome. While there are those who may view the church as a symbol of how far we have progressed from a more austere and inflexible past, or as a representation of where we stand today as a shining example of extravagant welcome, it is neither of those to me. With respect to the past and appreciation for the present, I see the church not from the perspective of history or even current events, but in the light of the future, with its endless potential to fulfill what were once lofty ideals and are now simply blueprints for things yet to come. If, as they say, children are the future, I look forward to entering adulthood with the United Church of Christ, whose members' unfailing faith and idealistic hopes will never settle for the past tense. The UCC has already held noted importance in its past years for me and for countless others, but its true significance has yet to be revealed in the radiant future of our church.

Roma Panganiban, Central Atlantic Conference

ONE STEP, ONE CHANGE

"Kids are supposed to play HERE?"

There I was, a suburban middle-class white teenager on the broken-glass-littered concrete surface of land between some of the worst "housing projects" in the country, Pruitt Igoe in St. Louis. Our small youth group had gone there to lead some activities for children through one of the mission houses in the city. It was as if God, through the church, had literally picked me up from the grassy yard of my comfortable home and plunked me down in an alien world where children were growing up in poverty, expected to play among the glass shards.

It was a conversion experience that changed my heart and my life. It is entirely possible that without God's church moving me out of my suburban comfort, I might have been a very different person. And though I quickly learned I could not "solve" poverty, I went into social work and then into ministry, where I have continued to try to press the church not only to act in charity but to ask the hard question of why any of God's children live in poverty in our time. To this day, I believe that God's people can put an end to the poverty that daily kills thousands.

Jane Fisler Hoffman, Illinois Conference

GOD NEVER LEFT ME

As a kid, I went to our UCC church every Sunday, no questions asked. At least until sixth grade, when I started thinking for myself and wondering, why go to church? The more I wondered, the more I doubted God and everything I was being taught to believe about God. I became an atheist because I believed that I, not God, was in full control of my life and that humans, not God, determine their own fate. Christianity was just superstition and meaningless ritual. So, even though it disappointed my parents, I quit going to church.

A year later, my father began feeling stomach pains. He visited doctors, who put him through test after test, and even though they all turned out negative, the pain only worsened. On top of that, he was having trouble keeping food down and he was losing weight. As a last resort, he had a biopsy. The surgeon opened his abdomen to see what was wrong, and she discovered pancreatic cancer. But it was so far advanced, she could only close him up and tell us that Dad had only a few months left.

In desperation, we sought a cure. Doctors tried experimental radiation. Friends suggested special diets and natural medicine. Relatives held prayer services, asking God for a miracle. But Dad was dying, slowly and painfully.

In the midst of this, people and ministers from our UCC church came to visit Dad, bring casseroles for the family, and spend time with us kids so Mom could work and care for Dad. And they came not once, but constantly. Even after Dad died, they were still there with us, through grief and beyond, staying close like family.

I was amazed. Why would people go out of their way and do that? I realized this was God at work. Like Job in the Bible, I could doubt and reject God, but God never left me. Throughout my father's ordeal, God was constantly present in the church people who reached out. They became the loving hand of God.

I was so impressed I returned to church, went through confirmation, and later became a minister. And today it still amazes me how people can love and do kind things for other people, even when they don't have to. That's God's touch.

Charles C. Buck, Hawai'i Conference

FUN AND FAITH

When we are sitting around the lunch table at school and the topic of church comes up, some of my friends roll their eyes and start brainstorming what excuses they can use to get out of church this week. But I catch the eye of one of my friends who goes to the same church I do, and we just laugh because we know what we're both thinking: I can't wait until Sunday morning!

The high school youth leaders at my church have an amazing ability to make the entire church experience both fun and meaningful, something I think many of my friends have not yet had the chance to experience. Our group recently got back from a retreat at one of the camps around the area. During the course of the weekend, we played snow football, tug of war, danced, sang, had snowball fights, dressed up in silly costumes, had lip-synching contests, and even had a few silly-string and shaving cream fights. Overall, church retreats are some of the most fun weekends of the entire year. And yet, amidst all the fun, we all learned so much too. We learned about each other, about our leaders, and also about ourselves. Some of the topics of discussion were: discoveries I have made that have really influenced my faith, why bad things happen to good people, who might need a little extra help this holiday season and how I can show them Jesus through my actions, how people have helped me and taken care of me, and now how I can use these principles as I find people who now turn to me for help and care. There was time for self-reflection, and group reflection as well. New relationships were made and old ones renewed. I intercepted a pass and ran it for a touchdown, while learning lessons I'm not going to forget any time soon.

So when I'm sitting at our table tomorrow and one of my friends asks if my retreat this weekend was any fun, I'm going to remember the sore abs from laughing too hard, the great experiences, and I'll simply thank God I have such awesome classmates and leaders with whom to share those experiences.

Maggie Pierson, Minnesota Conference

A COMMUNITY OF FAITH AND LOVE

Our family moved to Sacramento, California, when I was in the eighth grade. My parents started looking for a church, and after a few months, mom found one that was just beginning. I well remember the first Sunday we went. It was a house on a regular street. Warmly greeted, we felt right at home. The church was the Parkside Community Church.

In a few years, we built our first sanctuary, fellowship hall, and classrooms. As a new church, it was important that the youth be in worship so it would look like many attended. We ushered and some were lay readers. Adults and youth worked together, and youth felt included and valued as members. Sunday evening, there was Pilgrim Fellowship where we wasted a lot of time and caused adults to go crazy; but we did service projects, performed a major play we took on the road, and experienced Christian community.

It was early in the fight for civil rights for blacks, especially in the segregated south, when our church held educational events and stood for the rights of all people. We hosted a Sacramento reception after James Meredith became the first black to attend Mississippi University. I was learning and experiencing that faith and Christianity challenge the injustices in our society.

I did not realize until many years later how very unique and special Parkside Community UCC was in the late 1950s and 1960s. Our membership included African American, Chinese American, Anglo, and Japanese American members. I simply assumed this was the way churches were.

Of course Parkside UCC wasn't perfect. We had church fights, we didn't speak out as much as we once had, and we weren't very good at evangelism.

How did God touch me in my teen years? That is easy. I know their names; I see their faces even now, more than fifty years later. Most of these saints have passed away; yet, it was and still is their love and the embracing community that made God's presence real to me.

Thank God for welcoming and including our family in a new church.

Alan N. McLarty, Pennsylvania West Conference

NEW FREEDOM

An experience that has changed my life was finding God. I was never much of a church-goer until I found the United Church of Christ. I absolutely fell in love with the pastors, the members, and the church itself. I was taught about the Bible and I was baptized and confirmed in that church last year.

I used to be timid and quiet and afraid to be myself. I didn't do many activities outside school. Now I have something to look forward to on Sundays instead of just sitting at home. The church choir is fun and boosts my self-confidence. I was afraid to sing in my school choir because of what others would think, but in the church choir I'm not judged and can just sing. I hope that everyone can find hope and comfort in God and a church. I know I did.

Jasminn Shultz, Ohio Conference

THE DOORWAY WE PASS . . . THROUGH

Growing up in Chicago, Sundays were always special to me. In the morning, I'd walk with my siblings to the most wonderful church in the world. We followed the railroad tracks for many blocks, methodically counting the rail spikes and stepping on each railroad tie until we reached the busiest intersection. There we'd have to cross that street and follow it a few more blocks to the corner. Maybe it was the excitement of getting to walk further than my normal two block radius, or the rush as I waved to the trains we passed that without fail would blow their horn in response, or the need to stay alert on that busy street so I didn't get run over. Whatever it was, once we reached that sanctuary, I felt immensely secure. I felt like I belonged and I felt like God loved me and would take care of me.

On my tenth birthday my family moved to Oklahoma, and we left behind grandparents, aunts, uncles, cousins, and *my* church. Our family moved again many times, and with each move, my mom would find us another church, but I never felt particularly close to God. As I moved through adolescence, it seemed that God just wasn't there for me. If only I could go to *my* church again, maybe everything would be better.

When I was fifteen we took a trip back to visit relatives and we had time to visit the "old neighborhood." I made it a point to find my old church too and see if God was still there. It was just as I had remembered it, including the aroma of candles mixed with hardwoods and incense that I fondly call "church smell." In the distance I heard the sound of a train. I don't know if it was God talking to me, or the first sign of maturity that hit me, but I realized that I didn't need this place to know God. After all, God's presence was in the fragrance, the sound of the train, and even in my heart. I found God again in that moment and I invited God back into my life.

Cindy Sattler, Pacific Northwest Conference

SHAPING MY SPIRITUAL JOURNEY

As a teenager, I had many events that helped shape my religious beliefs and personal faith journey. What I realized is that without help from other people—my teachers, my parents, my friends—I never would have formed my current way of thinking. It is impossible in life to do things all by yourself. God is revealed in many ways; one of these ways is that God surrounds me with many people who help me with my spiritual journey.

One big way that God has helped me learn more about my faith is by guiding me as a delegate to my denomination's General Synod. It was an experience that allowed me to meet new people in the United Church of Christ and have them teach me more about what God can do and has done through these united people. It was an experience that I will never forget, and it let me network with many people that want nothing more than the best for me in my spiritual journey.

God shows me all the time that God answers my call. Whenever I need help, people appear in my life who can show me what I need to know or give me knowledge that allows me to make good choices.

Brad Jankord, South Dakota Conference

CELEBRATING GENERAL SYNOD

I've always believed in God. It's something that comes with the territory of being the daughter of a minister. Religion was never forced upon me, and I was free to explore every option and discover my beliefs in my own time.

Even though I'm a preacher's kid, my faith never took an active role in my life. I went to church until I was confirmed, and when it became my own choice, I stopped going, except for Easter and Christmas Eve. Sunday became one of those rare days I actually could sleep in, especially after working one day on the weekend and all the homework I had.

Then a few things happened in my life that made me reevaluate. The major one was that I attended General Synod with my mom during the summer of 2007. It was one of the most amazing and eye-opening experiences of my life. I became extremely proud of my faith and my denomination in those four days.

Synod changed the way I saw my church. I learned about all the ground-breaking things that the United Church of Christ has done in the past and is working towards now. I knew that Christianity didn't have to coincide with conservative views, but it amazed me that the UCC had been so liberal and outspoken for so long.

As a result, I examined my own faith. I really tested what I believed in against what I discussed with other people, and I began to know myself much better because of this. After experiencing Synod, I came home inspired to do more, and to share with others that there really are religions that are open and accepting—you just have to search them out.

Molly James, New Hampshire Conference

SAVED?!

When I was in high school, I loved *Kung Fu*. No . . . not the martial art . . . the TV show! You may not know it if you are less than fifty years old!

It was on in the early 1970s. A Buddhist monk wandered the Wild West and used his kung fu (only as a last resort, of course) on the bad guys he met each week. The rest of the time he was a gentle seeker of truth and spiritual path, having a lot of flashbacks to his training as a child in the monastery.

I started watching it at a time in my life when I was in between: in between childhood and adulthood, in between circles of friends, in between knowing what I believed and feeling that those beliefs didn't fit anymore. I felt like a wanderer on the spiritual path. But many of my "Jesus Freak" friends believed any one who was not a born-again Christian would not be saved.

The early '70s were the beginnings of an evangelical revival of Christianity. It was an easy fit for some of us: the passionate countercultural messages of Christianity resonated with the anti-establishment sentiments of the late 1960s hippie era. We wore our tattered blue jeans, long hair, love beads, and bare feet with pride as we preached the love of Jesus.

Then, I went home and watched the latest episode of *Kung Fu*. Something did not sit right with me. My friends would have said, "That TV show is making Buddhism look good, but those people aren't going to be saved!"

Stupid, right? It was just a TV show. But wait . . . thirty-five years later I understand that God was opening a door. God was speaking: "Barb, I don't *close* doors, I *open* them. My realm does not get *narrower*, it gets *wider*." Now I understand how God opens new doors and speaks in new ways in all times and places!

Barbara D. Doerrer-Peacock, Southwest Conference

I REMEMBER MY BAPTISM

I was fifteen, the oldest of the five or six kids baptized that Easter Sunday in Columbus, Ohio.

I remember my baptism.

Stepping into the baptismal pool, my white robe billowing around me as I entered the waist-deep water, I remember Rev. Frank Brosend, placing his right hand behind my head to hold me and his left arm for me to hold on to, saying, "I baptize you, my sister, in the name of the Father, the Son and the Holy Spirit," then tipping me back into the waters that echo Jesus' baptism, but also symbolize dying to sin and rising to life in Christ.

I remember my baptism.

American Baptists don't baptize infants. To enter the church through that sacrament, one first has to make a profession of faith, and so Baptist children are usually at least eight or nine before the rite. Traveling with my father in the Air Force, my family had not joined a local church, and so I was baptized at age fifteen, while the others baptized on that same day were several years younger.

I remember my baptism.

Adult deacons represented the church by helping us to dress for the baptisms, receiving us as we left the water, and welcoming us into our new life as full members of the church.

I remember my baptism.

The very tangible elements of water, and speech, and human touch all showed me God's presence, care, and eagerness to embrace me.

Ruth Garwood, UCC Coalition for Lesbian, Gay, Bisexual, and Transgender Concerns

FAITH THAT ENDURES

For me to talk about my youth and to talk about church is to make a confession: I am one of "those!"

All of my life I have gone to church. I never took a break. I never quit for a period of time. I didn't skip out during college. I have always gone to church. *I am one of those!*

I have gone when others have called us hypocrites. I have gone when societal forces have called us irrelevant. I have even gone when, for my generation, it wasn't the "cool" thing to do. I have gone when others have seen us as nothing more than dry bones.

I have gone because despite all of its frailties, the church has fed my soul. I have gone because others in the house of faith have nurtured me and guided me and cared for me. I have gone to hear the sometimes uncomfortable truth. I have gone to learn and grow and be challenged. I have gone and over the years experienced, personally, the new muscles and the new flesh growing on the "old bones." "Dry bones, hear the Word of the Lord."

But I am now more than fifty years of age and it occurs to me, more and more, that the church of today is not the church of my youth. And as nostalgic as I may get some days, it should not be the church of my youth. The church must speak in a voice that can be heard by the present and future generations.

As the preamble to the Constitution of the United Church of Christ says: the responsibility of the church in each generation (is) to *make this faith its own* in reality of worship, in honesty of thought and expression, and in purity of heart before God.

So my word to the youth of today is—*Make this faith and this church your own!*

Gene E. Miller, South Dakota Conference

JACOB, MY HERO

My childhood home was a dairy farm in Wisconsin. It had all the amenities of a mid-twentieth-century home, including a strong faith. My family was active in Beechwood United Church of Christ. As a teen I taught Sunday school and vacation Bible school, played organ for worship, and participated in the youth group.

My faith was something that I merely accepted and never questioned. It was rarely a source of conversation around the home, other than the impact of participation in the life of the church on a busy farm schedule.

As a teen I never saw myself becoming a pastor. A music teacher or a veterinarian, but not a pastor! I went to Lakeland College, graduating with a BS in education. The problem was that I was in a struggle with God. Like Jacob, God and I had very different ideas of the future. God was telling me to become a parish pastor, and I was convinced that I should be a band director. So I put together a plan. I would go to seminary and fail miserably and then go about my merry way directing high school bands. In the fall of 1968 I enrolled at United Theological Seminary of the Twin Cities. I was so confident that I would return to my previous vocation that I only took a leave of absence from the Kiel Schools, where I planned to return and resume my career as a band director.

During that first year of seminary, I, like Jacob, wrestled with God. I wouldn't give in and neither would God. Several times, a job in the music field came open or I got a letter from the Kiel Schools. I was confident I knew what my future was going to look like. God's vision would not be so easily changed. The moment of faithful truth came at the end of my first year at United Seminary when I was invited to be a part of the outreach ministry of a Minneapolis congregation. Through this opportunity for involvement I came to understand that God not only was calling me to follow the path of ministry but was also assuring me of the Spirit's presence as a partner on the journey. For me it was like stepping through a doorway and beginning an adventure it would take a lifetime to complete.

I have been following that journey for nearly forty years. I give thanks each day for a persistent God.

Wade Schemmel, Northern Plains Conference

HEALING HAPPENS HERE

It was in the mid 1970s when one of the elders in the congregation I was serving as pastor came into my office and said, "Russ, I think we need services for healing in this church." He also was a physician. He also had discerned that wholeness comes from far more than a bottle rattling full of pills. "I will look into it," I responded with a certain air of incredulity at Bob's unexpected request.

I really didn't know what to do. My seminary training had cut things like spiritual healing out of my neat theological package along with all the other miracle stories in the New Testament. There was no UCC Book of Worship with liturgies for anointing in those days, few helps in other mainline denomination's worship resources. Most of us mainliners had relegated such things to religious fringe groups and TV evangelists. So, first I had to recover theologically what I had abandoned, and I had to restore to my Bible things I had cut out. It was a life-changing conversion for me. God was working something new in me, thanks to a committed Christian physician and elder in the church. He and I together preached a dialogue sermon, approaching healing as a physician and a pastor, medically, biblically, and theologically.

I also had to develop a liturgy for anointing and healing, which in subsequent revisions has found its way into some of my publications. We started doing the rite monthly as part of the communion services, and that congregation more than thirty years later still carries on this ministry. Most people who came for the laying-on-of hands did it for others—acts of self-giving intercession for those who were sick. One Sunday another elder, a man of considerable wealth who owned a trucking firm that still stretches all across the nation, came to the chancel and knelt. "I'm coming for a young man who washes my trucks," he said. "He's been diagnosed with cancer." I cannot recollect that moment without tears, that a man of such means could kneel down and receive anointing and laying-on-of hands for his truck-washer. Dr. Bob and Elder Harold and a whole host of others brought me to where I wasn't, and I owe my eternal thanks to all these Christians for the ways in which God was working in me through them.

F. Russell Mitman, Pennsylvania Southeast Conference

WORDS OF COURAGE

God touched me during my teen years just as God does today—in slow and steady measure. There wasn't one amazing person or overarching incident; God touched/touches me in ordinary ways and occasionally places me in what seems like extraordinary circumstances.

I grew up in a small neighborhood UCC church north of Boston, Massachusetts. Next door to the church was a pharmacy/convenience store with a soda fountain—sort of the sixties version of a Starbuck's—where we would congregate following Sunday school. Probably as much wrestling with putting biblical teachings into action took place there as at the church.

About a year after confirmation and membership into the church, our pastor announced to the congregation that he and his wife would be seeking divorce. This was scandalous at the time. He hadn't broken any ministerial boundaries (we didn't use that terminology back then). Neither he nor his wife had been adulterous, they simply (though there's nothing simple about it) needed to end their marriage. The church leadership reacted immediately and called a special congregational meeting to call for his resignation.

Gathered at the pharmacy, the youth-fellowship leadership contemplated our pastor's plight, the overreacting on the part of the adults, the apparent injustice of the whole situation, the questioning around treatment of individuals in hard places; we pondered what action we should take. We decided as voting members of the church, we should attend the meeting and speak out. It came to me, as president of the Youth Fellowship, to be the spokesperson.

I do not remember one word I said that day, but I do remember praying before I rose that "the words I was about to speak would be acceptable in God's sight, our strength and our redeemer" (not the last time I would utter those words quietly or aloud). I did feel the presence of the Spirit that day, holding me steady, filling my mouth and the deep sense that we had been strong witnesses for justice.

Yes, there were adults who also stood in favor of supporting the pastor and his wife through this hard personal time. The vote was to affirm his ministry, and he remained with us for a good many years after the divorce. We, as teens, guided by the Holy Spirit, had taken a leadership role and helped to make a difference in the life of the pastor and the church.

Nancy J. Lawrence, Massachusetts Conference

RESOURCES FOR SHARING STORIES

6 THE WISDOM OF STORIES AND A FEW WORDS TO THE WISE

SHARING FAITH STORIES is one of the most meaningful experiences a person can have. Out of our own stories, the stories of our contemporaries and the stories that have been passed on to us—including those written in the Bible—we gain wisdom. From stories we gain wisdom for living.

Two aspects of sharing faith stories are equally and differently valuable. First there is the shaping and organizing a "story" out of what might have simply been random impressions or life elements that are not often discussed, such as gratitude, joy, doubt, or hope. This may take place in silent reflection or in a personal journal. Once a story is recognized, it becomes a foundation for further spiritual growth and, yes, for wisdom.

The next step is sharing a story with someone else, perhaps an individual, a small group or—in the case of the generous contributors in this book (none of whom asked to remain anonymous)—with many people whom the one sharing may never meet. A book can make a difference. Michelle Santiago's reflection testifies to how a book changed her life.

What follows in these next pages are some very pragmatic suggestions for identifying faith stories and sharing them. These suggestions are in the service of small group facilitators, youth ministry staff and volunteers, confirmation leaders, and mentors. Adapt, change, and amend these suggestions to fit your setting. Please take very seriously our cautions—they are the result of mistakes we have made!

We start with four "words to the wise":

1. Faith stories are not appropriate "ice breakers." That context automatically diminishes their importance and the informality of the setting often makes shy people miserable and vulnerable ones "goofy" or inappropriately humorous.

2. Never force public disclosure without adequate and clear instructions. These are the kind of instructions participants like to hear *before* they write or reflect. "After we write these prayers . . . we will each read them aloud . . . those who wish will read them aloud . . . we will pass them around and read each other's prayers anonymously . . . we will place them face down in the offering basket and pray silently.

3. Share faith stories, episodes or anecdotes, rather than "your whole spiritual journey." It is easier to look into a small window than try to unroll a detailed blueprint. A too-large scope freezes some people. Others, who for one of many reasons, including protecting someone else, need to eliminate some part of their life story, feel guilty because they cannot comply with the request. In addition, "spiritual journeys" are long, and in a group context the last couple of people to share will have the emotionally scarring experience of realizing that folks are getting bored!

   Frequent personal sharing develops a skill for it, gradually erodes anxieties, and allows the person having a bad day (and everyone does, including the leader) know that there will be another occasion to be more fully invested.

4. Don't do group therapy. In fact, most contexts for sharing faith stories ask for a response of gratitude and affirmation but rarely comment. Do be aware of an individual partici-pant's need for subsequent individual attention or further assistance that may be professional.

7   THE QUESTION

THE BASIS FOR ANY SHARING—whether written or spoken—is a meaningful and open question. A good question should not lead to a "Yes/No." response.

Question: *When have you . . . ? Remember a time . . . ? What's a similar experience . . . ?*

Not a wise question: *Have you ever . . . ? Can you remember . . . ? Has this happened to you . . . ?*

A good question should not have one answer that is more ethically acceptable than another.

Question: *What's a risky behavior in which you've engaged . . . maybe you recognized it was risky at the time or only understood that it was later?*

Equally valid answers could be—"I crossed the street when I was five" or "I threw up after lunch every day second semester of my eighth grade year."

Not a wise question: *Do you respond physically to stress by going to the gym or cutting?*

A good question can be answered by every single participant honestly. A good question is as welcoming as the United Church of Christ tries to be.

A really good question can be answered by every single participant in *more than one way*—typically one answer is more revealing, but another answer is also true, though a little more cautious in a group context. These are not bad and good answers. Both are good, honest, and faithful. They are simply at different levels of vulnerability.

Question: *What is a wonderful nonphysical gift you've received?*

Everyone has at least one answer: "My talent for art, my grandmother's love before she died, my first solo driving in my parent's new car, my acceptance by my friend after I 'borrowed' money from his locker without asking, God's love and forgiveness . . ."

Most people could answer this question in more than one way: *What is a wonderful nonphysical gift you've received?* "The freedom my folks gave me to make a huge mistake, quitting the music lessons that were so much a part of me to get a job so I could buy more clothes." Or "my parents' trust when I was twelve and they let me baby-sit my newborn sister."

These are genuine responses and they both witness to a strong parent/young person relationship, but the first one is a more personally vulnerable response.

The best questions ramble a bit. A question that hopes to start people sharing at a deep level should take a few minutes to soak in.

Question: *What is one deeply touching Christmas experience you have had? It doesn't need to be the absolutely best experience and it doesn't need to be church related, though it might well be. It might be happy or sad, and it might not have been meaningful to anyone but you, but it should be something that is important. It could be a Christmas Eve candlelight service, or the expression on your fourth grade teacher's face when you knit her that scarf with all the holes, or the way your parents were careful to share Christmas Day the first year after the divorce, or what it really felt like to be an angel in the pageant. You could probably come up with a different answer each day if I asked you three days in a row. That's all right—it doesn't need to be perfect, but for right now, what comes first to your mind."*

The "rambling" in this question has several different elements.

The question invites the listeners to come up with "stories," discreet moments. It provides safety by saying it does not need to be religious (for those who have slim church background or who have a powerful family, nature, or school experience).

It provides perspective by admitting that it might not be the "ultimate" story so that group members don't freeze up trying to pick what they hope the leader wants to hear.

It specifically invites "sad" so that the first Christmas after the loss of a companion animal is an acceptable answer and it specifically invites "happy" so that no one thinks that sensitive or spiritual automatically means teary-eyed. It does not invite "funny," because people will always strive to be humorous, if it is an option, in the attempt to please others and will forget the initial personal "Aha" that came to mind.

There are examples suggested that jumpstart the thinking and they intentionally come from different levels of vulnerability.

Finally, initial free association is encouraged over deliberation.

One way to offer an example is for the leader to respond first. The risk in that strategy is that the group will attempt to replicate the level of vulnerability in that story—shallow or deep. Some young person also may say, "Well, nothing that interesting has ever happened to me." It usually works better to offer at first a little list and then for the leader to speak midway through the group. That sometimes helps to get things back on track if the group has veered off topic.

The answer to a questions can be shared in very small groups by going around the circle. Others don't comment or respond while each person is speaking. This can become a lovely gathering activity. It is often facilitated by passing a Native American "talking stick," a candle, a smooth stone, or some other physical object.

In a large group or, if this ritual for speaking is associated with reconciliation after group conflict, a good alternative method is sharing in pairs or triads for five minutes and then asking for any stories that might be shared with the whole group. There are other more intentional versions of sharing faith stories as a longer group activity.

GROUP ACTIVITIES FOR SHARING FAITH STORIES

8   A CIRCLE OF CONVERSATION

THE GROUP SITS IN A CIRCLE and counts off by twos. A #1 and a #2 speak with each other, responding to a single question. Then a bell is run and each #1 moves counterclockwise to sit with the next #2 and so on, so that everyone has a new partner. The #2s do not move. If a pair are in deep conversation, a #1 can move past that pair to the next available #2 and they will not move until the next round. No pair should stay together for more than two rounds.

Give about four minutes—two minutes for each person to answer. Ask four questions, and then, with the fifth partner, share a story that someone else has shared. Remind participants at that time to think about confidentiality and consider which of the stories that they have heard are appropriate to share. This is hard to do and helps people seriously consider how we talk about one another in other contexts. At the conclusion, spend some gentle time collecting insights from the experience. The whole process takes about forty minutes.

Why is this not an icebreaker? This is a serious time of sharing stories, and the regularity of the pattern helps those who hate the chaos of finding someone in a large room and/or being the last chosen. In that form of game, people are often more concerned about plotting the next switch than listening to the current partner. In the circle of conversation each participant also has an opportunity to learn something very interesting about several different people—not only the ones with whom she or he would normally sit. There is great comfort in anticipating the next partner and deciding on the level of vulnerability.

WHAT ARE SOME POSSIBLE QUESTIONS?

About me. This set of questions I ask with all ages in helping people write their memoirs.

Place. *Share with your partner a geography of your childhood. What was something about the outdoor world when you were younger that was important to you? It could be an awesome camping experience or your favorite swing in the backyard. It could be a grandparent's garden you visited rarely or your daily spot to wait for the school bus. There are probably lots of these places, but share one that is meaningful to you and comes quickly to mind.*

Person. *Share someone older than you who has influenced you for good—a mentor. Let's leave parents out . . . but pick a teacher or coach or scout leader or neighbor or grandparent or a friend's older sibling. Again, there are probably several of these people—I certainly hope there are—but pick one and tell your new partner something about him or her.*

A pet or a passion. *This time you have a choice. Tell your new partner either about a companion animal who means or meant a lot to you (it may be an animal who has died) or share a passion—a hobby—it could be ice hockey or knitting or going to animé conventions. If you have both—a pet and a passion— make a decision about which one is more important to you.*

A thin place. *The Celtic people called the juncture where the everyday and the mysterious meet a "thin place." Share a thin place of yours—it could be an amazing dream or the way a prayer seemed to be answered, a sense of déjà vu (of something having already taken place), or simply the way you felt completely at peace somewhere. If you've had surgery, it might be the feeling of coming out of anesthesia or it could be the sensation of closeness you have with someone who has died. There is no right or wrong on this question—whatever seems most mysterious to you, share with your new partner.*

Retelling. *As Christians we "tell the stories" of others, many of them stories about Jesus. With your final partner of this circle of conversation, please share briefly a story you have heard around this circle. You have heard someone tell you about a place, a person, a pet or a passion, and a thin place. Consider seriously whether you think someone would like you to repeat his or her story and choose one that you are confident is "fair to share." Of course, this is also a test of whether you were really listening to the other person or trying to figure out what you were going to say (you may laugh)!*

About worship. I often ask these before a group is going to plan a "Youth Sunday."

Holy days. *What is your favorite holiday at worship? Can you remember a particular Christmas Eve, Easter sunrise service, Pentecost, Maundy Thursday, Church School Sunday, pageant, World Communion Sunday, or—you name it—that means a lot to you? Describe what happened.*

Part of worship. *What is your favorite part of the worship service and why: hymns or other music such as praise songs, sermons, baptism, communion, prayers—whatever. This could be a Sunday service at church or it could be worship at camp or a retreat. I don't mean the whole service (though you might end up talking about it). Try to identify a single part.*

It bugs me. *What happened once or happens often in worship that turns you off, makes you uncomfortable? Are you bored in a prayer, feel awkward when people hug during the "peace," re-*

sent multiple offerings . . . ? Maybe you've felt excluded some-where or uncomfortable at a wedding or funeral. Whatever comes to mind . . .

I was moved. *When have you been deeply moved in a worship context—it could be a Sunday morning or a holiday, at a camp or on a mission trip. Maybe you felt like God was talking directly to you, or you felt just amazingly close to everyone, or you got shivers hearing a soloist. Share with your new partner a worship experience that moved you.*

Retelling. *(same as above)*

Many gifts, one Spirit (1 Cor. 12:12–13). This is great right after Christmas.

Wonderful! *Share with your partner an absolutely wonderful gift you received before the age of [half their age—if they are fifteen or sixteen use eight, etc.]. It could have been a Christmas gift or a birthday gift, a thank you gift, or just something totally unexpected. Share what it was and how you felt about it.*

I'm a giver! *When have you felt truly wonderful about giving something away. It could be a present you planned or saved for, something of your own you gave away, or money, muscles, or time for a mission project.*

Awkward! *When have you felt awkward about gift giving? Maybe you had to open a package in front of people or had to thank someone for a gift you didn't really like (or made that obvious and know you hurt someone's feelings). Maybe you felt obliged to give a gift and you really didn't want to do it or you brought a gift to a birthday party and the person obviously didn't like it . . . or maybe it wasn't as expensive as the other presents. Any way you take this— share an awkward gifting experience.*

Not stuff! *Share a meaningful "nonphysical" gift you have received—maybe someone's trust or respect . . . maybe a chance to be with someone or go somewhere . . . maybe it's a gift from*

God, such as one of your talents . . . or even some extra time you had with someone that you knew was gong to die. We all receive nonphysical gifts all the time, so you have lots of choices. What is one that comes to mind for you this evening?

Retelling. *(same as above)*

9   HOLDING A STORY IN MY HAND

VISUAL AND TACTILE CLUES are far more important to many people than oral messages. Promptings for spoken and written sharing of faith stories work well if they are balanced between verbal questions and suggestions and those that emerge from or involve some form of visual or "hands-on" experience.

SAND GARDENS

A form of tangible contemplation developed by Joan Jordan Grant of the Alcyon Center on Mount Desert Island, Maine, to facilitate sharing faith stories is Sand Gardens. The leader spoons a covering of white gardener's sand in as many plastic plates as there are participants. In the center of the room are bowls or baskets containing small objects—such as sea shells, pine cones, keys, glass balls or marbles of different colors, cloth, crayons, miniatures, bells, birthday candles, and the like. The invitation is to place these objects in the tray (to play with them) and then to describe how this collection of objects portrays something about the participant's life.

Here are some possible words of introduction to this activity

You may want to choose an object for each one of your years—a symbol—and create a life spiral, or you may want to use different objects to create a narrative memoir of your life.

You may want to find something in one of these baskets that can represent you. Place that in the center of the tray, like the hub of a wheel, and put symbols of different things that are important to you around the edge. These could be people, pets, activities, hopes . . . anything.

Or you may want to place some of these objects in the tray to describe or make a picture of who you are and what your day is like today. There is no right and wrong. Some of our trays will be fuller than others!

For those who love art, this activity is a blessing; for those who fear art, the impermanence of a tray of sand (unlike clay or a picture) that can be infinitely changed and then taken apart at the end of the activity is freeing. People speak more freely when they are holding small objects in their hands.

Finally, invite each one to take something from the sand tray as a small talisman.

PICTURES

Photographs are a wonderful way to reflect on the past. One suggestion is to invite young people to bring in a photograph of themselves or to bring one for every two years of life. Unfortunately there is always a young person who lives with folks who do not take doting photographs of him or her across the years. These situations range from difficult home settings to youngest sibling syndrome. The sheer damage this does to this person is not worth the easy sharing of all the others (see Rom. 13:13f).

Here is the gentle alternative. Scatter on a table a wide range of photographs of people doing things. Use old and younger people, different seasons, and different family combinations. Bring real photographs rather than magazine pages. A good number would be four times the number of people in the group.

Here are some possible words of introduction to this activity:

Look at all these photographs of people you don't know . . . well, mostly . . . and find one that reminds you of an experience you've had. The people are different and the place is different, but there is just something—even something just in the corner of the picture—that reminds you of yourself. After everyone has one we are going to take two minutes in silent reflection and then go around the circle and share the reason you chose the picture you did.

A variation of this activity uses the faces of Christmas cards —especially in the summer. The directions are the same. For Protestants Christmas is certainly the season of the greatest visual expression, and Christmas cards are as close as we come to icons.

Finally, a collage of "my life"—and that broad an invitation is probably best—can be done as a silent activity with magazines, fabric trim, cloth, cotton balls. When this is a verbal activity there is so much suggestion—"Hey, Courtney, this could represent your little sister!"—that people lose focus and don't explore personal metaphors.

GOD IS LIKE A LIGHTBULB

"God is like a lightbulb" is a prayer writing activity that can also be used to share faith stories. Fill brown sandwich bags with miscellaneous objects. Provide five more than the number in the group. These bags may contain a miscellany of natural and manufactured items. The participant "parables" his or her object in a one sentence or more of self-description and may go forward to a story or stop at that point. Common items would include bark, sea shells, toilet paper, bar soap, computer mouse, sea glass, credit card, autumn leaf, spoon, and so on.

Here are some possible words of introduction to this activity:

We will open the bags and respond "My life is like . . . " or I am like . . ." or something similar. I'll try it—"My life is like. . . duct tape because I'm always holding things together for people." "I am like an apple—my skin is thin and I bruise easily but I've got lots of seeds for new things inside." "My conscience is like a GPS—I know the way to go but I don't always follow." "I'm like a feather because my mind just drifts away in class, but also, if God is like loving wings, I want to be a feather on God's wing helping to shelter someone."

This activity floats back and forth from humor to sensitivity. Relax if it moves out of control and try again in a written format.

10   WRITING FAITH STORIES

THE WONDERFUL THING about writing activities is that everyone has a response—not only the most extroverted participants. Although only a few may share what they have written, each member of the group has his or her writing to reflect upon at a later time, or even to share with a friend or the group leader. It is also the case that, in a discussion, each comment links to the immediately preceding remarks and often folks forget their initial response. The piece of paper or the index card reminds them of those "first thoughts."

Many folks blog and write live journals, perhaps more than keep handwritten journals. A topic for discussion is the switch to less-than-completely-private journaling that the Internet invites. The best written activities for a group do not, however, involve bringing in pieces from a live journal or even writing stories at home and bringing them to youth group. This feels too much like "homework!"

In fact, people are often self-conscious about their abilities to write, particularly if that is not one of their academic talents. Youth group writing should be something quite different.

Introduce a writing activity or game with directions like these:

On your index card I'm going to ask you to respond to this question. I won't give you very long, so nobody can polish what he or she writes. We are looking for free association and an immediate response. Spelling? 4get it! Grammar? JK! Nobody—I mean nobody—will look at this but you. I will ask for volunteers to share what you've written but it's not "expected." Just enjoy!

Depending on the time frame, a written faith story sharing can be as simple as *"the time I went to"* and one sentence. With more time it could be a full short story.

The exercise "God is like a lightbulb" works as a written exercise.

Please take the object out of your brown paper bag and write one sentence or more . . . .my life is like an onion . . . a padlock . . . a sea shell . . . a cell phone . . .

A grab bag in which each person receives a different memory to write about is an effective way to avoid competitiveness in writing. Essay contests and college essay anxiety are responsible for a contemporary black hole of writing confidence. The grab bags strips might read something like these:

Write about a birthday party you remember—yours or someone else's.

Write about a memorable Christmas morning—it could be memorable because it is happy or sad.

Write how your life is like a reality show.

Write about a piece of clothing that you love/d—now or at a younger age.

Using nonpermanent surfaces to write on helps everyone forget blue books! Index cards are wonderful. Paper plates make a fabulous writing surface for remembering a family meal. Writing about a meal is a favorite activity for young people and it connects to the meal we share with God, Holy Communion.

Describe who is around the table and who is missing . . . what is eaten . . . what your feelings are . . . perhaps even share some dialogue, if you remember it.

Judith Barrington in *Writing the Memoir: From Truth to Art* (probably the best "how-to" memoir book available) has a writing exercise called "Mealtime Memoir." It is similar to this one, but using a paper plate takes away the stress.

Writing on a table covered with paper is a wonderful way to have an individual-in-community experience. People will be less personal, but this is a perfect way to share after a mission experience. The large format works for those people whose natural creative expression is artistic rather than verbal. Drawing a story as a single picture, a comic strip or a storyboard appeals to these folks, and the casual nature of the brown or white paper roll relaxes those who are uncomfortable with art. Julia Cameron and Mark Bryan in their well-known *The Artist's Way* suggest an exercise for "Creative Unblocking" that involves drawing a cartoon of oneself in procrastination mode.

What do you do that wastes time so that you don't have it for the things that really matter to you?

On the extremely personal end, writing one word on a "stress ball" with a marker is a subtle way to release tensions! There are a wide range of other writing-surface possibilities. Sidewalk chalk around the church is one. Banana skins are a great surface—the writer is likely to "peel off' some layers of protection. Instead of just signatures, *I remember* with frosting pens makes a beautiful cake at the end of the year (be sure to photograph it!). *I remember* . . . with fabric markers on a T-shirt makes a welcome gift for a youth group leader.

Of course, youth group members or adults can write to one of the writers in this book. An e-mail to Lovetotellstories@ gmail.com will be forwarded on to the particular author. No e-mail address—not the "fan's" nor the author's will be shared in either direction.

11   USING THIS BOOK TO SHARE FAITH STORIES

ONE WAY TO USE *God in My Life: Faith Stories and How and Why We Share Them* is to use the five chapter themes as five gathering times for a group.

You can ask participants to read a chapter each week and choose a story that is meaningful to them during that week. The time frame suggests a personal story rather than a generalization from the "book story." It's also unnecessary to pick one's "favorite" book story. (There is often an expectation of what "ought to be" the best story.)

An even simpler method is just to offer each topic and a question to share. Participants can respond to the stories in the book if they have read them, but those who have not been able to do so are not embarrassed.

Grace Encounters. *When have you suddenly been overtaken by a sense of God's presence—through an unexpected meeting or new experience, in a dream, or at a time of heightened emotion?*

Into the Wilderness. *What place in nature gives you a feeling of spiritual connection? This could be in "wild" nature or watching the stars from your own backyard.*

For All the Saints. *Who has influenced you in powerful and positive ways . . . a teacher, a coach, a friend, a neighbor, a brief acquaintance? (For this one time, let's leave out parents, but you could choose a grandparent.)*

Blessings for the Edges of Life. *When have you been on the "edge"—of an emotional, social, or justice-related experience and received some new understanding or blessing?*

The Church Family. *On what occasion have you experienced a community of support—this could be church but it could also be a team, a group of friends, a musical group, a youth group?*

Some of the following engaging sentences or paragraphs from *God in My Life: Faith Stories and How and Why We Share Them* can be prompts for personal journaling, story sharing, or general discussion. You may simply ask, *How do you respond to this person's words?* or *When have you had an experience like this?*

Some suggested questions follow each quotation and may be more specific, although the intent is still to be general enough that every participant is included. Remember always to ask *When have you . . . ?* Rather than *Have you ever . . . ?* (to which someone will answer "No.")

After discussion, you may want to return and read aloud the whole essay. Feel free to choose other paragraphs from the many stories in this book or ask a youth group member to choose a paragraph for the following week. These are chosen from the youth stories—although not all the youth stories. There's no intention to shun the adult contributors—in fact, a light hearted question might be, *Which grown-up (in the book or in the chapter) was an adolescent most like me?*

SOME SAMPLE QUOTATIONS:

I think God wants all of us to be open to meeting new and different people and all the joys that come from these experiences. From my time in Tanzania I learned that God's love can be found in the most unlikely of places, even in something as simple as a game of soccer. (Alex Cook)

When have you been able to connect with other people because of a simple shared activity?

It was the community and the sense of love among the people that intrigued me. As time wore on I began to attend my own church more frequently and I became more involved. I soon discovered that the church that my friend attended had very different theological perspectives than the church that my family attended; nevertheless, the community and sense of love were the same. (Chelsea Bicknell)

When have you visited in another religious community? or *What do you respect most about another religious group . . . either a Christian denomination or another world religion?*

I looked at myself and I wondered: Who am I? Why? I was quiet because I was scared; I read because I had no friends; I wanted a guy because I had no confidence or self-love. Then, I found love. Not from a guy, but from God. (Courtney Monzyck)

Free associate and answer Courtney's question—who am I? or *When have you turned to God for guidance and confidence in responding to a relationship?*

During high school I experienced a huge transition: instead of working towards the career I was planning on pursuing since I was five, I became more proactive in the UCC, and more advanced in music—my two big passions. In pursuing these, though, I had to give up a lot of time with friends, family, and just relaxing to enjoy life. (Kevin Peterson)

Remember a time when you have given up family, friend, and fun time to focus on a passion. What was it? or *How do you bring God into your post-school/vocational choices?*

I feel like I personally have gained a measure of confidence in my relationship with God, because here was this atheistic kid and I was able to help him a little bit. That's made me feel like God really is able to affect some things. (Henry Stone)

When have you reached out to someone who needed a friend (long ago or recently)?

The news of Kevin's death [killed by a car bomb in Baghdad] frightened me into thinking I'd always be alone. I'm not a person who tends to cry a lot. In times of great stress or tragedy, I hold all of my feelings inside me. It's one of the worst feelings in the world. With Kevin's death, I became even more stressed about my life and what the future holds. (Matthew Leong)

Remember a time you felt particularly fragile, vulnerable, lonely. What were the circumstances around that time? How did it work out?

When I almost passed out in choir one evening, it was Shirley who immediately began to care for me, throwing orders at me to sit down, drink water, and eat something. I admire her youthful energy, positive outlook on life, and the amazing power her smile holds. (Tricia Earl)

Who is an older person—not related to you—who has cared for you in a supportive way?

One day after church, during my sophomore year, Wiebke came up to me and asked me if I wanted to help lead a retreat for middle schoolers. I was really hesitant, because there would be no one else there that I knew, so that really scared me. But Wiebke kept pushing me, and soon, she had basically signed me up without me really saying yes. (Emily Bass)

When have you done something new—without knowing anyone else involved? or Who pushes you into doing new things?

Sitting in the stiff, cold pew, I bent my head in an attempt to hide my tears. It was not easy for me to be in a church because

of all the things I had experienced at my "home church" the previous two years. (Sarah Frische-Mouri)

Sometimes we feel betrayed in school, youth group, team,
club contexts. Remember a time when this has happened and
what helped you. (This may be the most difficult of stories, be-
cause most of us group facilitators dislike talking about the
frailty of human institutions, like churches. It's easier to focus
on the good side of community life. Wonderful conversations
can emerge from being this vulnerable about church authority
in a youth group context. Nancy Lawrence's story, with which
the book ends, is a powerful testimony. Nevertheless, leaders
should consider whether this is an appropriate discussion in a
particular context.)

Though we all come from Christ-based beginnings, we've all
ended up being very diverse, religiously. Two of us are Catholics,
one devout, one doubting. Several are conservative Christians,
very dedicated. Quite a few are more liberal Christians, some
liberal in their belief in Christ, others certain, but open to other
religions. One has dabbled in Buddhism, some look at
Hinduism, many of us meditate. One decided very recently that
she is an atheist, and a few would identify with agnosticism.

While many of those invited are heterosexual, a few are not.
Many are peacemongers, but some still support the war. Some
make sure to recycle, some try to use less gas, some don't notice
that kind of thing. (Jennie Wachowski)

Jennie is describing a Thanksgiving meal. Remember a time
when you have been at a table with an unusual group of people.
What happened?

You see, being born to a drug-addicted, teenaged mother who
couldn't have cared less about me, and bouncing around from
friend's house to friend's house for more than a year, until being
taken in by my godmother, who would later adopt me, I like to
think that it was ME that pulled through, that I am the master
of my own fate in the sense that I am the only one responsible

for who I am today, and that God played a cameo role in it all. But the truth is, without God, things would have been very different for me. (John Allen)

When have you suddenly realized that more than YOU was dealing with a situation? or Write your background in one sentence the way John does.

There was also a different interest in the falls [Victoria Falls] on behalf of the visitors, an interest that did not exist in respect to the rural poor. God was present in each situation, but it seemed that people's attention was more focused on the falls, a touristy destination where spending money on souvenirs was easier than volunteering time for a cause. (Meredith Jackson)

When have you been struck with the kind of discontinuity that Meredith describes? How did you feel . . . did it cause you to do anything?

Laying in my bed, eyes straining in the darkness, the light burned in my eyes. It was dark, but everything was so clear and bright. That small light, that small flame, that vast darkness was a shot to the head, heart, and soul. And as I awoke, I became something different. I felt as though I was immersed in a new world. (Elizabeth Becker)

When have you had a transcendent, mysterious, or almost unreal experience? This could be a dream . . . the sense of the presence of someone who wasn't really there and perhaps is dead . . . a clear internal warning in traffic . . . a visual experience that seemed to glow . . . a sense of déjà vu . . .

God had influenced the words and phrases. And it was God who used me to unknowingly write a sermon that was inclusive of all marital relationships. You see, the first sentence is, "When the love between *two people* is so strong, they get married." (J. Alan Williams)

J. Alan's unexpected "youth sermon" led to his taking a stand on a social issue. When have you taken a stand?

Some of the topics of discussion [at a youth retreat] were: discoveries I have made that have really influenced my faith: why bad things happen to good people, who might need a little extra help this holiday season and how I can show them Jesus through my actions, how people have helped me and taken care of me, and now how I can use these principles as I find people who now turn to me for help and care. (Maggie Pierson)

What would you really like to discuss and where is a safe place for you take your issues?

<table>
<tr><td>12</td><td><h1>MAKING SCRIPTURE
STORIES OUR OWN</h1></td></tr>
</table>

Scripture study is always in some sense "making scripture stories our own." That happens in two different "directions." On the one hand, we read a story in scripture and try to get into the skin of the person who is portrayed—to understand that person's dilemmas and that person's faith. Trying to understand biblical characters on their own cultural terms is reading responsibly.

On the other hand, sometimes we are reading the text and suddenly recognize a character who is like us and with whom we empathize. We want to know everything about that character and come to a deeper level of self-understanding in the process. John Allen's story "Gideon" is a wonderful example.

On a spectrum in between these two positions are ways in which we "holy play" around with the stories in scripture to learn more both about the Bible and about ourselves. Some of that can involve storytelling, which is not unlike the Jewish practice of midrash.

One way to make a biblical story our own is to contemporize it—to find a parallel to the central situation and perhaps some of the details and retell it in our own cultural terms. This is done respectfully and in full recognition that the contemporary story is not the text but a way to experience the text. The raw material we use to be able to do this exercise is, in fact, our own faith stories—the struggles and hopes and many experiences of God's presence in our lives.

A quick contemporary retelling that involves acting is a skit. A similar more reflective version is writing a screenplay of the biblical story and then reading it aloud or acting it. Because a screenplay actually needs to write out the various "camera shots," the group members participating in writing it are literally thinking about the *focus* of the story.

Improvisational portrayals of individual biblical characters imagine their personalities as well as often more than one biblical incident. A monologue (by Martha or Stephen for example) can be improvisational or prepared. An interview (of Jeremiah or Lydia) engages two people in mutual improv, as one comes up with questions and the other with plausible answers. An e-mail from Paul or from the angel in Revelation to the youth group or youth group's church involves serious background reading and significant reflection on the issues of the modern faith community addressed.

Expanding the scripture story in its own time also actually allows participants to consider others through their own experiences.

What happened yesterday—what is the back-story for the woman at the well?

What will happen tomorrow? Imagine the ten lepers, nine of whom did not thank Jesus, in ten years' time. What would they say? How would they explain themselves? This particular story is very flexible because ten people can exercise their imaginations and their storytelling skills without any one being in competition with an interpretation!

Whenever we tell faith stories in our communities—the scripture stories that have been told in oral tradition and stained glass, in song and novel, in sermon and movie, or our own stories of struggle and blessing—we are, in fact, exercising storytelling skills. We let the text live and expand rather than boiling it down to more concentrated dogma or doctrine. Stories open us into new experiences with God because even the oldest ones always have new plot twists, prequels, and sequels. We can, like the popular children's books of several years ago, make our own endings!

13 SHAPE-CHANGING FAITH STORIES

FAITH STORIES, faith stories, faith stories. It's getting boring. Even—stories, stories, stories—can be a little dull.

So here is a possibility. Invite participants to think of a story about themselves that they have shared at some point: maybe a "thin place," a "saint" who has touched their lives, a time that prayer felt vivid and real, an ethical decision, or an experience with death—of a friend, relative, companion animal, neighbor. Once one story is firmly in mind, invite them to "tell" it, probably in written form, but it could be oral . . .

as a newspaper article . . .

as a television newscast . . . who might be interviewed?

as an e-mail . . . or a text message! to a friend . . .

as a conversation with a grandparent . . .

as a screenplay for a movie . . . who would "play" you?

as a prayer . . .

The faith story can change shape just once for some simple sharing from the different format. The text message is particularly fun. A participant can also take a single personal story and tell it several ways.

If each person does three or more changes, then a further conversation will develop about the differences themselves and how we change our story without really changing it to adapt to different situations. A comparison of different "tellings" of the same story in different gospels or the different "tellings" of the creation story can contribute to this conversation.

The list of "shape-changes" can be as long as the leader's imagination. Ending with sharing the experience as a prayer deepens the discussion. The prayers are almost always shorter than other forms and simpler.

14   USING FAITH STORIES IN WORSHIP

FAITH STORIES CAN BE USED in youth group worship and in congregational worship. Here are ten wonderful ways to share them.

1. Shared reflections on events can be recast into sermons. The ideas of a number of youth group members can be shared by one representative.

2. Prayers written out of personal experience can be shifted into a communal expression and each person can consider how particular each experience is and yet how similar it is to the situations of other people.

3. Writing new lyrics to familiar hymn tunes is great fun. "The Mission Trip" song becomes an enthusiastic or poignant way of remembering, and, because music is so intimate a medium, it shares the experience at a deeper level with those who did not participate.

4. The story of a particular event or of the youth group year can be told in a PowerPoint presentation. Often youth group members have more facility with that form of story telling

than do many adults. Choosing music to complement the visual impact involves more of the group in worship planning.

5. The re-created contemporary versions of "making the scripture one's own" can become a children's sermon, the way the morning scripture is read, or a portion of the sermon.

6. The individual memories of youth group members (for example of things they are grateful for on the Sunday before Thanksgiving), each condensed to a single line, can create a powerful litany to which each youth group member contributes. The group itself can decide on the shared congregational response line.

7. One of the faith stories from this book can be read in worship and several young people can respond to its message.

8. A Sunday (perhaps in October to honor Francis of Assisi) that focuses on blessing animals can have a youth-led time of sharing stories of companion animals who have died and what they meant. This brings a tender focus to a frequently boisterous time.

9. Often the Sunday after Christmas has a casual atmosphere. A gathering of Christmas memories can become a way for individuals to contribute a brief story to an interactive sermon. A particularly lovely way to "pass the peace" on this intergenerational occasion is to have people pair off and share a personal Christmas story as a way of wishing "Peace on Earth."

10. At a Good Friday retreat for youth, a quiet time could include each person sharing a favorite story about Jesus, not referring to it, but telling it as if it's new to the others (which it might be). This mirrors how people gather at visiting hours for someone they love who has died, and is a gentler way to receive the full impact of the Good Friday loss than focusing on the passion-details of torture and execution.

15   STORIES WE BUILD TOGETHER

YOUTH GROUPS AND CONFIRMATION CLASSES do many things together. The storytelling possibilities are numerous and exciting. There can be many stories that come from a mission trip, a lock-in, a homeless supper, a mosque visit, a ski weekend, the candlelight walking of a labyrinth, the National Youth Event. Sometimes those stories are told for one another and for congregations or association meetings in creative ways. There are wonderful newsletter articles and youth sermons that emerge from significant times.

Admit it—there are also some drab newsletter articles written by the person who was not able to get out of the room as fast as everyone else and there are sermons that touch on the facts of an experience and the inspiring moments but gloss over the funny and touching little memories along the way! And, of course, there are also deeply moving youth occasions that are not of interest to the "rest of the church" and so do not receive the same attention.

The best way to save these small memories is to invite remembering in advance of an experience. A leader can give every participant an index card and invite him or her to jot down one thing that happens (or one thing a day). There might be a specific assignment, such as the following:

Remember one person you see at the shelter—his or her face, age, posture, expression. If you can speak to him or her—wonderful—but, if not, just try to make a mental portrait of someone who often may feel very forgettable.

On return read each of these cards and hold each person remembered in prayer. As Sharon Encabo Seegmiller suggests in her story in the book, the young people will remember these faces for a long time.

Everyone just remember one single line that someone says. You don't even need to remember who said it!

On return, throw the cards into a grab bag and pull them out, reading them like a script. It will be hysterical! Another way of sharing them is to write each line on a strip of white paper like a headline and tack them on a bulletin board. Maybe some photographs can illustrate these unexpected phrases.

When we come back [or tomorrow morning], you will each be filling out a card that begins, "I thought of God when . . ." This can be just one thing or maybe several things. Don't overthink it! We can all use "I thought of God when we said grace at dinner!!!" You don't need to write these experiences down. Just trust your subconscious to be keeping track of this small mental assignment.

At the end of this time, their "subconscious," their "spirits" will provide so much to their writing hands that most groups have a hard time stopping.

Individual reflection after an experience is also a wonderful way to share group faith stories. A "circle of conversation" could share these questions:

What was the most fun—just plain fun—you had during this experience?

When did you feel most challenged (give possible examples)?

What is one thing you learned about someone else or yourself during this experience?

What do you think you will remember most—this answer may be the same as one of the ones above, or it may be different.

Skip the "retelling" question and share together the variety of things remembered.

Reading Maggie Pierson's faith story about her youth group's retreat is a discussion starter for thinking back on an experience together. Read it aloud and then ask: *How would we tell about . . . the way Maggie does?*

There is one way to share faith stories in the middle of an experience. This works well during a lock-in. In an unlocked office have an open laptop with "Our Youth Group Lock-In Blog." Everyone will write at least one short reflection during the night. They are free to take the computer to the sanctuary or on a night hike or into the sleeping bag room, but no one keeps it more than fifteen minutes. This implies trust of the young people. Just to help with that, we suggest that this computer not have Internet access. This sidesteps the temptation to check personal correspondence.

The conclusion of a youth group year is a wonderful time to share stories. Review not only highlights but also little memories. Avoid asking about the "best" thing that happened. There will be a majority opinion, which will immediately underline the "left-outness" of a person who was not part of that experience. It's better to ask:

So many meaningful things happened this year—big and little . . . give some examples—let's go around and share some small wonderful detail about this year in youth group.

There are many ways to do this kind of retrospective—pictures as well as words are important. Always be sure that the details are treasured as well as the big events.

One set of questions might use the senses:

What's the most interesting thing you saw this year?

What's the most interesting thing you heard this year?

What's the most interesting thing you ate (lots of laughs here) *this year?*

Then switch it around—*Surprise—I'm not going to ask what did you touch . . . but what touched you?* Because this will move to a deeper level—they probably won't notice that you skipped over the sense of smell!

16   A FEW FINAL WISE CRACKS

THERE ARE ALWAYS some comments that just don't fit in any-where else!

TEENAGERS LOVE TO TALK ABOUT THEIR CHILDHOOD

Life reflection is not just an activity for older people. Adolescents love to tell stories about their childhood—which may seem very distant. They are honored by being asked about younger years because it implies that they are no longer "little kids" and be-cause it means that adults are assuming that they have worked through and overcome some issues that were intense earlier.

Here is an example from a youth group retrospective. It's a simple story—certainly not one that is identified as "tragedy":

"When I was in the fourth grade I was always in trouble be-cause I didn't really think anyone would care for me unless I was a clown; then I got a best friend and that changed the way I felt about myself. Even though my best friend has moved away, I haven't lost that self-confidence."

In fact, adults often find it hard to judge what is actually a more difficult story to share. Getting picked up for drinking at an after-game party may seem much more serious than admitting that one never did sleepovers because of fear of bed-wetting, but in fact . . .

Giving young people a chance to share the triumphs and traumas of their younger years has its own value and becomes a bridge to sharing contemporary stories.

THERE ARE CIRCLES OF SAFETY AND CARING

Most of this book is about sharing in a wide variety of group contexts—from the gracious authors who have shared themselves with anyone who picks up this book to the youth and intergenerational groups who may share some of these activities. Confidentiality should always be mentioned. It is never obvious.

There are a variety of other groups that are defined by their increased level of safety. They can be valuable not as a replacement for youth group but as an addition.

Covenant groups. These include any group that formalizes the confidentiality and limits the group for a particular purpose and probably for a limited time (to avoid becoming a clique).

Support groups. These include any group that has a similar issue—recovery from a risky behavior, surviving similar difficult situations, responding to a cultural concern (here might be language barriers, weight issues, newcomers, PKs—preachers' kids, etc.), racial or ethnic backgrounds.

Age-specific groups. For some kinds of sharing a narrower age range is helpful. For example eighth graders have *some* empathy for high school seniors, but high school seniors may need a time to share their academic and vocational issues, and eighth graders may need to not hear "we've always done it this way," which, of course, happens in youth group just as much as anywhere else.

Gender specific groups and orientation-specific groups. There are many issues that young women or young men feel more comfortable discussing in a group of gender peers. The best resource for this issue is the wonderful volume *Doing Girlfriend Theology —God-Talk with Young Women* by Dori Grinenko Baker. It is wonderful, of course, for young women, but its insights can also be used with young men.

Gay, lesbian, bisexual, transgender and questioning youth have very particular kinds of stories. On occasion they may want to explore other issues in each other's company. Ruth Garwood, the executive director of the UCC Coalition for Lesbian, Gay, Bisexual, and Transgender Concerns, asked if she could write in this book something that was not "her issue" and we were delighted with her reflection on baptism.

GOOD AND NOT-SO-HELPFUL HUMOR

Laughter opens the heart. A group of people of any age that laughs together is a group with trust. A leader who can share gentle self-deprecating jokes and chuckle at his or her own expense is a blessing to any group.

In the sharing of faith stories, however, humor has a very modest role. No one should ever laugh at the story of another without an explicit invitation. The humor that is popular in contemporary society runs to humor of exaggeration and specifically humor that exaggerates and mocks differences—gender and orientation, ethnic backgrounds, mobility concerns, and learning disabilities. Even in groups that are careful about these concerns, weight issues, nonathletic interests and body build, often called "geekiness," are still often considered fair game. There is a two-fold damage in this kind of humor—for the person directly targeted and for the person repeating socially learned behavior and then realizing how hurtful it is.

When have you made a fool of yourself? What's the funniest situation you have ever experienced? Those are plausible questions. Most people are not skilled at the timing that creates humor, and though they remember funny experiences, they find it hard to describe them so that others laugh.

And that doesn't matter. The laughter in the youth group bubbles up from the funny things that always happen when good friends who trust one another are doing things together.

17   CONCLUSION

I love to tell the story of unseen things above,
of Jesus and his glory, of Jesus and his love.
I love to tell the story, because I know 'tis true;
it satisfies my longings as nothing else can do.
(A. Katherine Hankey, ca. 1868)

WE DO LOVE to tell the stories of faith—how God is found in our lives and in the lives of biblical characters, who become models of how to live and how *not* to live. Before they were told as stories, they were lived by real people.

We tell stories to ourselves, who may know them best, because we are hungering and thirsting for them. We tell our stories to others. The great healing method of the Twelve Step Recovery program is the telling of one's story. We are healed, encouraged, strengthened, and guided by stories. We collected stories from seventy contributors, hoping that they will be a means of grace.

God is still speaking in our stories, through our stories, and when we listen to the stories of others.

There is another old song, an African American spiritual tune, with words ascribed to John W. Work and best known through the Fisk Jubilee Singers:

Go, tell it on the mountain, over the hills and everywhere.
Go, tell it on the mountain that Jesus Christ is born.

It was the favorite song of our father and grandfather Russell E. Snider, who was born in eastern Tennessee at Boone's Creek, not far from Knoxville, where the National Youth Event will gather. Russell was a wonderful storyteller and we received our love for oral sharing of faith stories from him—though with Russ's stories people rarely could identify the boundary between factual "truth" and the truth of tall tale!

Russell died in the interval between these two Knoxville National Youth Events and we rewrote his favorite song for his funeral with a number of new verses and this refrain:

Go, tell it on the mountain, over the hills and everywhere.
Go, tell it on the mountain that Jesus Christ is raised!

Go, tell it . . . The purpose of this book is not only sharing the wonderful stories it includes and encouraging those who read it to share their faith stories. It is also to "tell it," to pass it on. That may take the form of recording the oral histories of older members of our congregations, grandparents, or folks living in neighborhood assisted living facilities and nursing homes. It may involve learning about the faith stories and traditions of peoples from around the world. Learning how to tell stories well is a skill that involves practice and timing. A storyteller could come to a youth group and teach the basic elements.

Finally, even as we learn to tell stories, we also learn responsibility about what and when and with whom to share our stories and the stories of others. Gossip is the most suspect of storytelling modes, and it is one with which we are all acquainted. The letter of James says some very true things about the dangerous "tongue" that, like a fire, destroys many good things in its path.

Go, tell it . . . and listen to it. Listening to the stories of others is so important. Thank you for reading these stories because your sharing them with us in this way is a blessing.

Index of Contributors

Index of Subjects